A World Champion's
Guide to Chess

Praise for *A World Champion's Guide to Chess*

Any chess player will find guidance in this professional introduction to the mighty game of chess.

—HAROLD DONDIS, *The Boston Globe*

Susan Polgar is a legendary grandmaster who has proven herself to be a player, trainer and author at the highest level. Everyone can benefit from her insights and knowledge in chess.

—GRANDMASTER BORIS GULKO

A chess prodigy at the age of 4, Susan Polgar has since become a worldwide chess superstar. After more than 30 illustrious years in chess, she now reveals the renowned training system that helped her. It will help you, too.

—GRANDMASTER LEV ALBURT,
3-time U.S. Champion, chess Hall of Famer,
and award-winning chess author and columnist

GM Polgar's pioneering contributions have secured her a permanent place of honor in the history of chess.

—ROBERT JOHN MCCRARY,
former president, U.S. Chess Federation,
and editor of The Hall-of-Fame History of Chess

Susan Polgar has enjoyed phenomenal success first as a player, then as a teacher and mentor to a rising generation of chess players. I am pleased to see that with this book she is sharing her winning methods.

—TIM REDMAN, PH.D.,
former U.S. Chess Federation president
and UTD Chess Program Director

Susan Polgar is brilliant, beautiful, and brings a touch of class to any event. She is an inspiration and role model to girls around the world. Susan is a true champion in her actions and words!

—BARBARA A. DEMARO,
managing director, United States Chess Trust

A World Champion's Guide to Chess

STEP-BY-STEP INSTRUCTIONS FOR WINNING CHESS THE POLGAR WAY

by Susan Polgar and Paul Truong

Random House
Puzzles & Games
New York Toronto London Sydney Auckland

To my children, Tommy and Leeam
—Susan Polgar

To my daughter, Brittany, and my son, P.J.
—Paul Truong

Please address inquiries about electronic licensing of any products for
use on a network, in software or on CD-ROM to the Subsidiary Rights
Department, Random House Information Group, fax 212-572-6003.

This book is available for special discounts for bulk purchases for
sales promotions or premiums. Special editions, including personalized
covers, excerpts of existing books, and corporate imprints, can be
created in large quantities for special needs. For more information,
write to Random House, Inc., Special Markets/Premium Sales,
1745 Broadway, MD 6-2, New York, NY, 10019
or e-mail specialmarkets@randomhouse.com.

Visit the Random House Puzzles & Games Web site:
www.puzzlesatrandom.com

First Edition

0 9 8 7 6 5 4 3 2 1

ISBN: 0-8129-3653-1

Library of Congress Cataloging-in-Publication Data is available.

CONTENTS

INTRODUCTION

My First Chess Experiences

I discovered the game of chess purely by accident when I was not quite four years old. While exploring a closet in search of a doll, I found some funny-looking figurines that looked like horses, castles, and a queen's crown. I asked my mother what they were, and she answered, "They are chess pieces. When your father comes home tonight, he will explain how to play with them."

It was through my father that I started to learn the basics of chess. He made the game so fascinating that I became deeply interested. Later my two younger sisters, Judit and Sofia, also learned the game and became very strong players. While I was still only four years old, I competed in the chess championship for girls under eleven years old in my home city of Budapest, Hungary. Although I was by far the youngest participant, I ended up winning the championship with a perfect 10-0 score! That was the beginning of my long and successful chess career.

During the past 30 years, I have been fortunate enough to accomplish quite a bit. I won my first World Championship (girls under sixteen years old) when I was twelve. I became the highest-ranked woman player in the world at the age of fifteen and have been ranked among the top three women in the world for the past twenty years. I participated in four Chess Olympiads (team championships), in 1988, 1990, 1994, and 2004, winning five Gold medals, four Silver medals, and one Bronze medal in team and individual competition. My sisters and I ended the Soviet Union's total dominance in Women's Olympiads. In 1991, I became the first woman ever to earn the Men's Grandmaster title. In 1992, I won my next two World Championships (World Blitz and Rapid Championships). In 1996, I won my fourth World Championship, becoming the first World Champion (male or female) to win the triple-crown in chess (World Blitz, Rapid, and Traditional World Championships).

What This Book Will Teach You

In this book I would like to share with you what I have learned and what has made me a successful player. This book includes not only methods that I have learned when I was growing up but also exclusive training methods that I have developed and used to train thousands of students over the years. An exclusive pattern recognition chapter will help you understand the foundations of dozens of patterns that will recur constantly in your games. Recognizing these patterns will let you see checkmates and other combinations three, four, five, and even six moves ahead.

In my lectures to parents, coaches, and young players across the country, I strongly recommend exactly what I have put in this book. I have come to realize that in the United States, too many players are not being taught properly. Too much emphasis is placed on the opening and not enough on other areas.

I highly recommend that beginners and intermediate players work mostly with tactics and endgames and solve tactical exercises every day. Tactics and endgames are the foundations of chess. Opening study is important only at much higher levels such as expert, master, and beyond. It is enough for beginner and intermediate players to understand only the basic principles of chess openings.

All the puzzles in this book are my original compositions. I feel these are the most important ideas for players to know. I am also working on more advanced puzzles to follow in a future volume.

How to Use This Book

To get the most value from this book, record the time it takes you to solve each puzzle by making pencil notations in the margins or in a separate notebook. Also note whether or not you've been able to find the correct move. When you have finished the entire book, go back and solve the puzzles again. Then compare the times and results. You should be faster and more accurate the second time. Repeat the same procedure a third time and see your solving time improve.

My father used to say: "Repetition makes a master. Repetition makes you a better chess player." And he was right. Solving thousands of puzzles really helped me become the player that I am today. The point is not to memorize the actual positions but to remember the ideas, to recognize the patterns. Chess is largely a matter of pattern recognition. The more patterns you know, the better player you will be. It is said that an average grandmaster has a mental library of about 20,000 patterns, which includes tactical, strategic, and endgame patterns. The main aim of this book is to help you build your own library of ideas.

THE ESSENTIALS OF CHESS

THE BOARD AND PIECES

The Chessboard

Chess is a fun and cool game. But before you can start playing you must know how to set up the board and pieces. It is quite simple, so don't worry. Let's go through it step-by-step.

There are 64 squares on the chessboard. There are eight squares horizontally (from side to side) and eight squares vertically (from top to bottom). The squares are laid out in alternating dark and light colors, as shown.

In order to keep track of what happens on the board, we use the coordinate (algebraic) system of recording moves and positions. With this system we assign a letter and number to each square. This lets you record a game by noting the location of each piece after every move. This system is based on combining a letter from a to h and a number from 1 to 8.

- The columns of vertical squares are called **files** and are designated by the letters a, b, c, d, e, f, g, and h.
- The rows of horizontal squares are called **ranks** and are designated by the numbers 1, 2, 3, 4, 5, 6, 7, and 8.

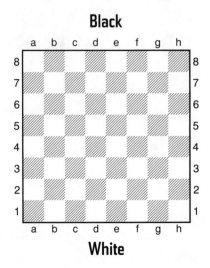

When referring to coordinates, remember that the letter always goes before the number. For example, the square below is called d4, not 4d.

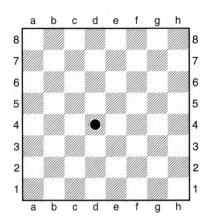

The square below is a6.

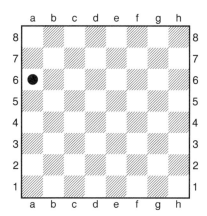

The square below is g4.

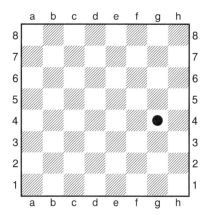

Remember: The board must always be set up with the light square h1 in the right corner closest to the player with the White pieces and the dark square a1 on the left side.

Files, Ranks, and Diagonals

Files are the vertical lines of squares. There are eight files, designated by the letters a, b, c, d, e, f, g, and h.

Below is the b-file.

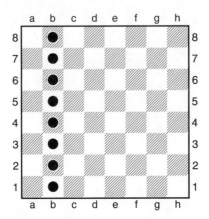

Below is the d-file.

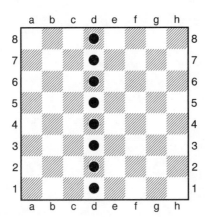

Below is the f-file.

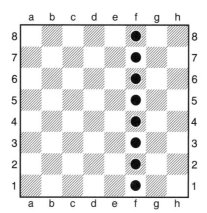

There are also eight ranks. These are the rows that extend horizontally across the board. White sets up the White pieces and pawns on the first and second ranks; Black sets up the Black pieces and pawns on the seventh and eighth ranks.

Below is the fourth rank.

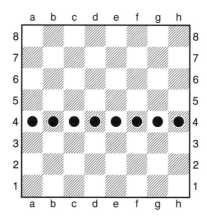

Below is the sixth rank.

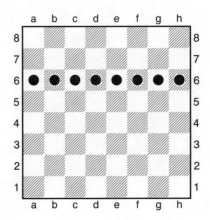

Below is the first rank.

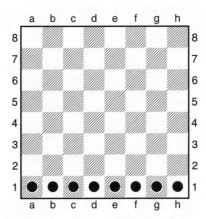

Diagonals are lines of connected squares of the same color slanting across the board. The bishop moves along diagonals. The following example illustrates the light diagonals a6–c8, a2–g8, and d1–h5.

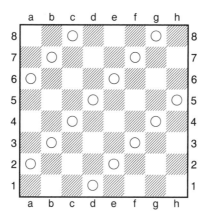

The following shows the dark diagonals e1–a5, h2–b8, and h6–f8.

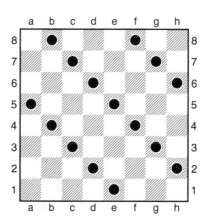

The Pieces

Each side has one king.

Each side has one queen.

Each side has two rooks.

Each side has two bishops.

Each side has two knights.

Each side has eight pawns.

White's pieces always start on the first rank. Black's pieces always start on the eighth rank. The White pawns are placed on the second rank (h2, g2, f2, e2, d2, c2, b2, and a2). The Black pawns are placed on the seventh rank (h7, g7, f7, e7, d7, c7, b7, and a7).

- Rooks start on the a- and h-files: White's on a1 and h1, Black's on a8 and h8.
- Knights start on the b- and g-files: White's on g1 and b1, Black's on g8 and b8.
- Bishops start on the c- and f-files: White's on f1 and c1, Black's on f8 and c8.

- Queens start on the d-file: White's on d1, Black's on d8.
- Kings start on the e-file: White's on e1, Black's on e8.

The pieces have different values according to their mobility. These values, based on the lowest value of the least mobile unit, the pawn, are used mainly in calculating exchanges. Here are their relative values:

Queen (Q) = 9 points

Rook (R) = 5 points

Bishop (B) = 3 points

Knight (N) = 3 points

Pawn (P) = 1 point

King (K) = No points

Sound complicated? It really isn't. Take a look at this diagram and you can see how all the pieces are set up for both sides.

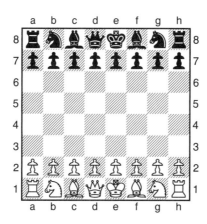

The Queenside and the Kingside

The squares with the circles, from the a-file to the d-file, belong to the queenside because the queens start on d1 and d8. All the other squares, from the e-file to the h-file, belong to the kingside because the kings start on e1 and e8.

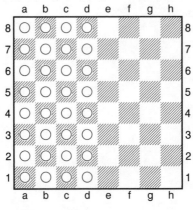

Queenside

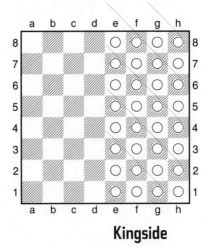

Kingside

HOW THE PIECES MOVE AND CAPTURE

The Queen

There are two queens in chess, each player having one of them. These are the starting positions of the queens for White (at d1) and Black (at d8).

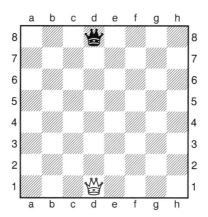

The queen is the most versatile, powerful, and valuable piece in the game. It is so versatile because it can move like a rook and a bishop combined. The queen is so powerful because it can move along files, ranks, and diagonals and can move any number of squares as long as there are no pieces in its path. The queen is most valuable because it is worth nine points on the table of relative values (see Tutorial 1).

In the diagram on page 14, the queen can move to any of the starred squares. As you can see, that includes all the squares on the d-file, the fifth rank, and the a2–g8 and h1–a8 diagonals.

In the next diagram, the queen can move to the squares h1, h2, h3, h4, h5, h6, h8, g6, g7, g8, f5, f7, e4, e7, d3, d7, c2, c7, b1, b7, and a7.

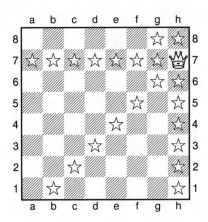

In the next diagram, the queen can move to b2, b3, b4, b5, b6, or b8 on the b-file; a7, c7, d7, e7, f7, or g7 on the seventh rank; a8, c6, d5, or e4 on the h1-a8 diagonal; or c8 on the a6-c8 diagonal. The queen can capture the Black rook on h7, the pawn on f3, the knight on b1, or the bishop on a6. But the queen may not move to g2 or h1 because the Black pawn on f3 is blocking its path.

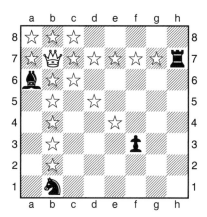

Remember: The queen is the most versatile, powerful, and valuable piece in chess.

The Rook

There are four rooks in the game, each player having two of them. The diagram below shows the starting positions of the rooks for White (at a1 and h1) and Black (at a8 and h8). The rook is the second most powerful piece after the queen. Each rook is worth five points on the table of relative values (see Tutorial 1).

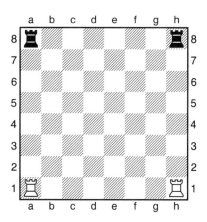

The rook moves along ranks and files, not diagonals, and can move any number of squares as long as its path is clear. A rook can capture any enemy piece in its path.

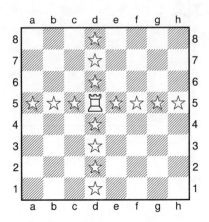

In the diagram below, the rook can move to the following squares: h1, h2, h3, h4, h6, h7, h8, a5, b5, c5, d5, e5, f5, and g5.

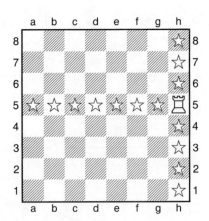

In the next diagram, the White rook on c8 can move to b8, d8, e8, f8, c3, c4, c5, c6, and c7. The White rook can capture the Black bishop on g8, or the rook on c2, or the knight on a8. The White rook may not move to h8 or c1 because it cannot jump over pieces that are in its path.

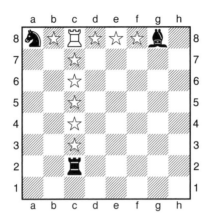

Remember: The rook is the second most powerful piece in chess after the queen.

The Bishop

There are four bishops in the game. Each player has two of them, one that moves only on the light squares and one that moves only on the dark squares. The first diagram below shows the starting positions of the bishops for both White, at c1 and f1, and Black, at c8 and f8. Each bishop is worth three points on the table of relative values (see Tutorial 1).

Each bishop can move only on the color of the diagonal it starts on, though it can move in any direction. That is, a bishop that starts on a dark square can move only on dark squares for the rest of the game, and a bishop that starts on a light square can move only on light squares for the rest of the game. A bishop can move any number of unobstructed squares and can capture any enemy piece in its path.

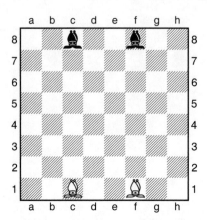

In the example below, the bishop can move only along dark diagonals because it is located on a dark square.

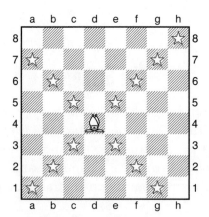

In the next example, the bishop is on the light square e4. That means this bishop can move only to the light squares c6, c2, d5, d3, f5, f3, g6, and g2. It may not move to a8 because a Black pawn is blocking its path. The bishop can capture the Black pawn on b7, the rook on b1, the knight on h7, or the bishop on h1.

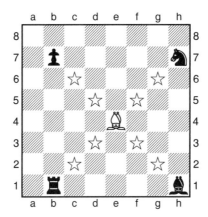

Remember: The bishop can move only on the same color diagonal that it starts on.

The Knight

There are four knights, each player having two of them. Below are the starting positions of the knights for White, at b1 and g1, and for Black, at b8 and g8. The knight is the most unusual piece in chess because it can jump over another piece. Each knight is worth three points on the table of relative values (see Tutorial 1).

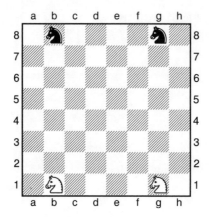

The knight moves and captures like a capital L. The knight must move to or capture on a square of the *opposite* color each move. In the diagram below, the knight (on a light square) can move to eight different (dark) squares: b4, b6, c3, c7, e3, e7, f4, or f6.

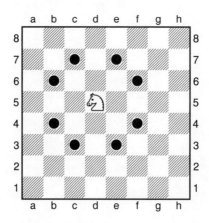

In the following diagram, the knight (on a dark square) can capture the Black rook on b3 or the pawn on c2 (both on light squares). The knight's mobility is most limited in the corner.

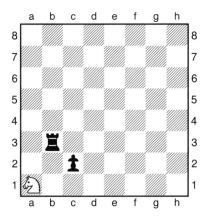

In this example, the knight (on a light square) can capture the Black bishop on c7, the rook on d6, the pawn on f6, or the pawn on g7 (all on dark squares).

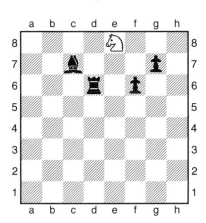

In the next example, the knight (on a light square) can move to the dark squares g1, g5, f2, or f4.

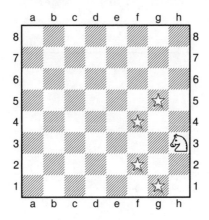

Remember: The knight always moves to a square of the opposite color.

The King

There are two kings. Each player has one. Below are the starting positions of the kings: for White, at e1, and for Black, at e8. The king is the only indispensable piece in chess. You cannot win without it, and therefore you must always protect it.

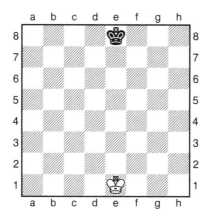

The king may move or capture in any direction, just like the queen (horizontally, vertically, or diagonally). However, its mobility is limited: it can move only one square at a time (unlike the queen, which can move any number of squares).

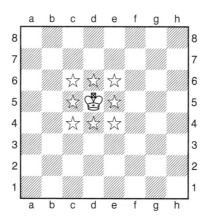

In the diagram above, the king can move to eight different squares: c6, d6, e6, c5, e5, c4, d4, and e4.

In the diagram below, the king can move to five different squares: a1, a3, b1, b2, and b3.

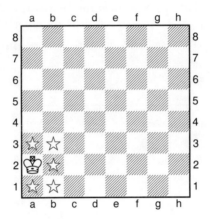

In the next diagram, the king can capture either the Black pawn on e4 or the Black knight on e6. However, the king may not move to a square that is attacked by an opponent's piece. Therefore, in the same example below, the king may not move to g5 or f4 because those two squares are attacked by the knight.

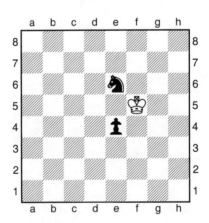

Sometimes the king can become very confined. In the diagram below, the king can move only to three possible squares: a7, b8, and b7.

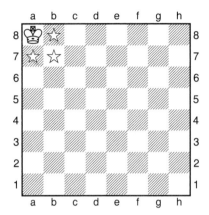

The king may not move to a square that is occupied by one of its own pieces or pawns, or to a square where it could be captured by an enemy piece.

The Pawn

There are 16 pawns. Each player has eight of them. Below are the starting positions of the pawns for White (a2, b2, c2, d2, e2, f2, g2, and h2) and for Black (a7, b7, c7, d7, e7, f7, g7, and h7). Pawns are the foot soldiers of chess. A pawn has considerably less power and mobility than any other piece. Each pawn is worth one point on the table of relative values (see Tutorial 1).

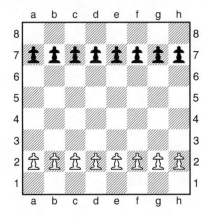

Remember: The White pawns always start on the second rank and the Black pawns on the seventh rank.

Pawns can move only straight ahead and only one square at a time, but there is one important exception. Each pawn on its first move can advance either one or two squares straight ahead. In this diagram the White pawn, making its first move from e2, has advanced to e3.

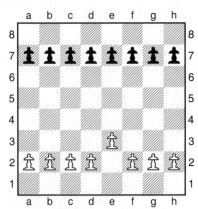

In the diagram below, the White pawn has advanced two squares, to e4. This two-square advance is possible only on a pawn's first move.

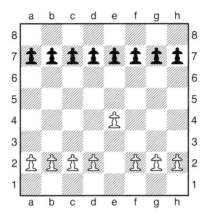

Even though a pawn can move only straight ahead one square at a time, a pawn captures *diagonally* one square ahead. The pawn cannot move or capture backward or sideways. In the example below, the White pawn can capture either the Black knight on d5 or the Black rook on f5, or it can move straight ahead to e5.

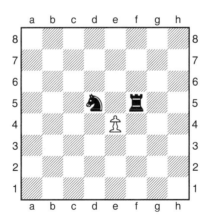

A pawn cannot move forward if there is something in front of it. In the example below, none of the White pawns can move because Black pieces and pawns are blocking them.

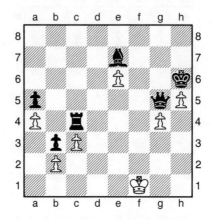

Remember: Each pawn, on its first move only, may move either one or two squares forward. After its first move, a pawn may advance only one square at a time.

TUTORIAL

III

OTHER RULES

Check

A King directly attacked by an enemy piece is in check. *The king must somehow get out of check immediately.* If it cannot, the game is over because of checkmate (see on page 32). In the following example, the White rook on e1 is checking (attacking) the Black king on e8.

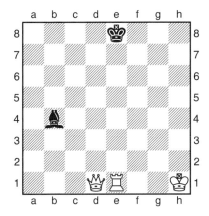

One way to get the king out of check is to move it to a safe square where it is not attacked, such as f8 in the diagram on page 30. The king may not move to a square where it would still be in check.

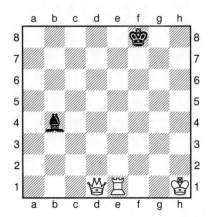

The move Kd8, however, attempting to escape from the check in the other direction, as in the following diagram, is *not* allowed, since the square d8 is attacked by the White queen on d1. *It is illegal to move a king into check.*

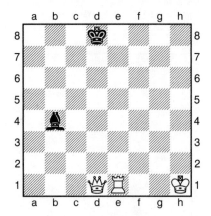

Another way of defending a king that is in is check is to "interpose" a piece between the king and the piece that is attacking it. Here the Black move Be7 protects the king from White's rook.

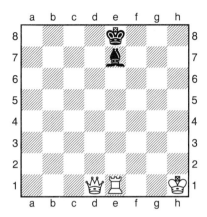

There is still another way to thwart a check, and that is by capturing the piece that is attacking the king. In the diagram below, you can see that the bishop has captured White's rook on e1, eliminating the piece that was checking the king.

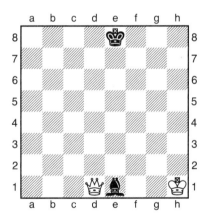

There are two exceptions: When a knight or a pawn checks the king, either the king must move or the knight or pawn must be captured. It is not possible to block a check given by a knight or pawn.

Checkmate

Checkmate is the goal of the game. Checkmate occurs when there is no way to move or defend a king that is in check. This means that the king has none of these three possible defenses:

- The king has no safe square to which it can move.
- There is no way to block the check by interposing.
- It is not possible to capture the piece that is checking the king.

In this example, the White rook on e8 is checking the Black king on a8. The king cannot move, there is no piece with which to block the check, and Black cannot capture the White rook. Therefore, Black is checkmated and the game is over. White wins.

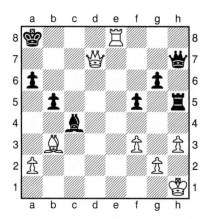

Remember: Checkmate is the goal of the game.

Stalemate

Stalemate occurs when a king is *not* in check but cannot make any legal move, and no other piece can move either. A stalemate is a draw and neither side wins. If a king *is* in check and has no legal move, it is checkmated and has lost the game!

In this example, it is Black's turn to play. His king is not in check and he has no legal move. Black is stalemated and the game is a draw. Neither side wins.

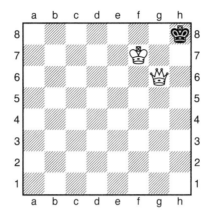

In the next diagram, White can capture the pawn on b5 with his king (the move is written Kxb5, with "x" meaning "captures").

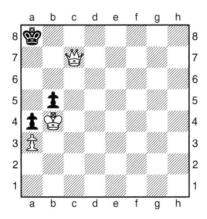

But after that move, shown in the next diagram, Black is stalemated. His king is not in check and neither of his pieces can move.

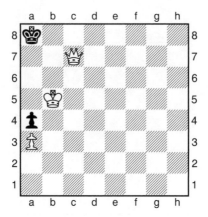

However, if the White king makes some other move, allowing the Black pawn on b5 to advance, stalemate is avoided, as in this diagram.

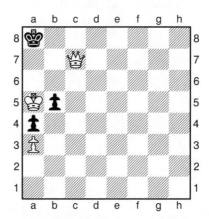

White's king has moved to a5 (Ka5) and there is no stalemate because the Black pawn on b5 can move to b4.

A stalemate can occur when there are only a few pieces on the board, as in the above example, but also when there are many pieces. In the following example, it is White's turn to play, but he has no legal move. Therefore, once again, a stalemate is the result and neither side wins.

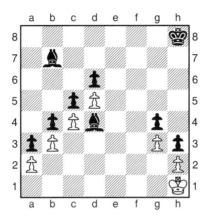

Castling

Castling is a special maneuver carried out by a king and a rook. It is the only time two pieces can move in the same turn.

The purpose of castling is to move the king to a safe place by moving it away from the middle of the board where it may be vulnerable to attack.

To castle, the king moves either to the kingside or to the queenside. The king and one of the rooks move simultaneously along the back rank. The castling move is written 0-0 for castling on the kingside and 0-0-0 for castling on the queenside.

In the diagram below, the kings and rooks are in their original positions.

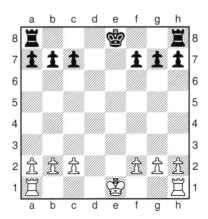

In the next diagram, White has castled on the kingside. The king moved two squares to the right, to g1, and the rook moved two squares to the left, to f1, on the other side of the king.

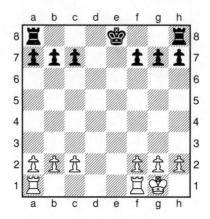

In the next example, Black has castled on the queenside. The king moved two squares toward the a-file, to c8, and the rook on a8 moved three squares to the other side of the king, to d8.

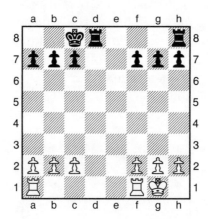

The Rules of Castling

There are some basic rules about castling to keep in mind:

- The king always moves two squares, either to the kingside or the queenside.

- The rook moves two squares when castling on the kingside, three squares when castling on the queenside.
- The king and the rook must be on their original squares and may not have moved. If one of the rooks has moved but not the king, you still can castle on the side where the rook has not moved.
- Castling is not allowed while the king is in check.
- The king cannot castle into check.
- The king cannot castle across an attacked square.

Remember: Castle as soon as possible to keep the king safe!

Pawn Promotion

Even though pawns have the least value of all the chess pieces, they have the unique ability to be "promoted" to any other piece (except the king). This remarkable transformation occurs when a pawn reaches the last rank on the opponent's side. This pawn has the *obligation* to immediately "promote" to a queen, rook, bishop, or knight. This is done by removing the pawn from the board and replacing it with the promoted piece. The following two diagrams show how White promotes a pawn from h7 by moving it to h8, where it becomes a queen.

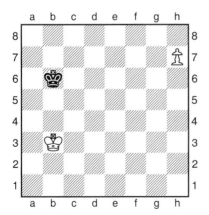
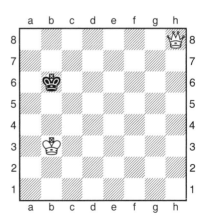

The next example illustrates how White promotes a pawn to a rook instead of a queen. In this case, promoting the pawn to a queen would result in stalemate. Therefore, the underpromotion (promoting to the lower value rook) would be better.

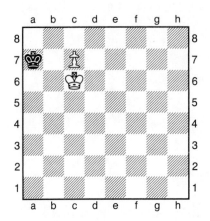
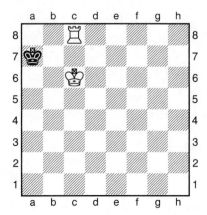

An important note: It is technically possible and perfectly legal to have nine queens, 10 rooks, 10 bishops, or 10 knights through pawn promotions.

En Passant

En passant (a French term that means "in passing") is another special pawn move. *En passant* occurs when a pawn advances two squares from its starting position and ends up adjacent to an opponent's pawn on the same rank. In this situation, the opponent has the option of capturing the pawn just as if it had moved only one square. The opponent must make the capture immediately or the opportunity to capture the pawn *en passant* is lost forever.

In this example, White will move the pawn from e2 to e4.

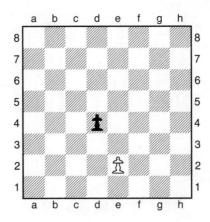

Now Black has the option of capturing *en passant* by taking the pawn at e3, as shown in the next diagram.

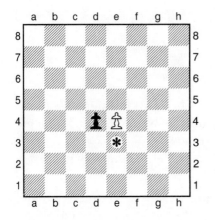 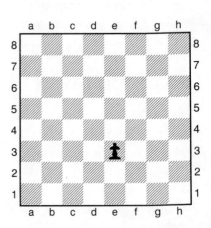

Important! If you choose to capture *en passant*, you must do so immediately. If you don't, you will never be able to capture that pawn *en passant*.

TUTORIAL

IV

THE NEXT STEPS

How to Win a Game

There are a number of ways to win:

- Checkmate your opponent
- Your opponent resigns
- Your opponent runs out of time

Checkmate your opponent

Checkmate occurs when a king is in check but 1) it has no safe square to which it can move, and 2) the check cannot be blocked, and 3) the piece that is attacking the king cannot be captured.

In this position, the White rook on h5 is checking the Black king. The king has no escape square, no Black piece can be interposed against the check, and no Black piece can capture the rook. Therefore, Black is checkmated.

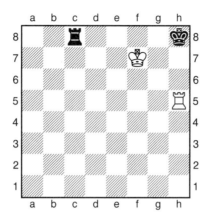

Your opponent resigns

When your opponent feels that his position is hopeless and he has no chance to win or even to draw, instead of wasting time he may choose to resign; that is, give up.

In the following example, White has two rooks and a king while Black has only a king. It is impossible for Black to win. In fact, White is about to checkmate Black in two moves by playing Ra7+ followed by Rb8#. It is perfectly reasonable for Black to resign rather than wait to be checkmated (the symbol "+" means "check" and the symbol "#" means "checkmate").

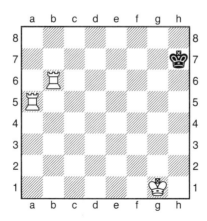

Winning on time

In tournament play, a clock with two faces is used to keep track of the time used by the players. Each player is given a certain amount of time to play a certain number of moves or to complete the game regardless of the number of moves. The player who first exceeds the allotted time without making the required number of moves or checkmating the opponent's king loses by time forfeit.

The time controls for various tournaments may be, for example, G/90 or 40/90 SD/60.

G/90 means that each player is given 90 minutes to complete the game. The player who first exceeds 90 minutes without completing the game regardless of the number of moves loses on time.

40/90 SD/60 means a player must complete 40 moves within 90 minutes. Once his 40th move has been made, each player has another 60 minutes to complete the rest of the game. Whoever has not made 40 moves in 90 minutes or has exceeded the additional 60 minutes after move 40 without completing the game loses on time.

Pace yourself wisely so you don't run out of time!

How Do You Draw a Game?

There are several ways for a game to be drawn:

- Agreement between the players
- Stalemate
- Repetition of the position three times
- Perpetual check
- Insufficient mating material
- The 50-move rule

Draw by agreement

The two players may agree to a draw if both sides feel that they have no real winning chances. In this example, each side has only a rook in addition to the king. The chance for either side to win is very remote and can occur only if one player makes a horrible blunder. It is reasonable for the players to agree to a draw.

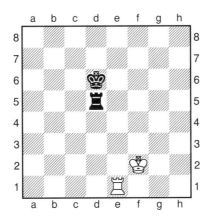

Stalemate

When the player whose turn it is to play has no legal move, the game is a draw by stalemate.

In this example, it is Black's turn to play, but none of the Black pawns can move and neither can the Black king. Since Black has no legal move, the game is a draw by stalemate.

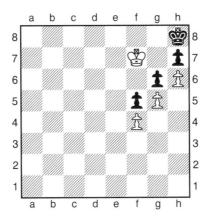

Repetition of the position

If the same position is repeated three times with the same player to move, the game is a draw by repetition. In this example, Black is threatening to checkmate White with Qh2#. White defends against the threat with Qg2. Black then moves the queen to b5 to attack the White pawn on a5, so White moves the queen to d5 to protect the pawn. Black then moves the queen back to b2 to threaten checkmate on h2 again, and White moves the queen back to g2 (the second occurrence of the position). If that position is reached for a third time, the game is a draw.

Follow the moves beneath the diagram. The White moves come first, in the left column, followed by the Black moves, in the right column.

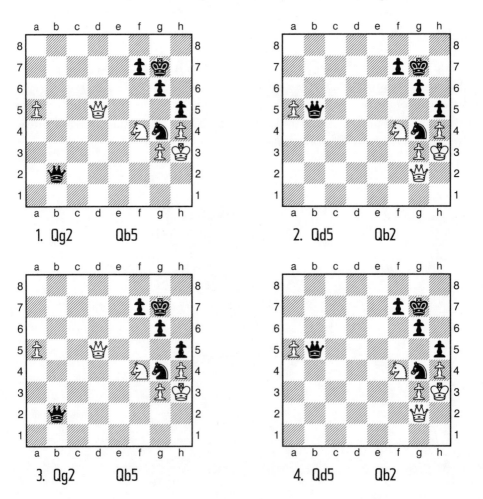

1. Qg2   Qb5

2. Qd5   Qb2

3. Qg2   Qb5

4. Qd5   Qb2

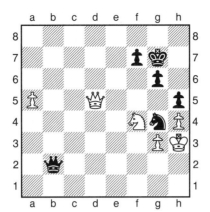

Here prior to playing on the board 5. Qg2 White can claim a draw.

Perpetual check

When a player checks the enemy king repeatedly and there is no way for the king to avoid the checks, the game is a draw by perpetual check. A player who has an inferior or losing position can try to get a perpetual check in order to avoid a loss.

Note that perpetual checks actually do not result in a draw until the same position is repeated three times. However, when the players face unavoidable perpetual checks, they often agree to a draw before repeating the position three times.

In this example, Black has an extra rook—a great advantage. Realizing this, White checks the Black king repeatedly on h6 and g6. The Black king cannot get out of the corner, so the game is a draw by perpetual check. When one side is about to reach the very same position for the third time, he/she can claim a draw.

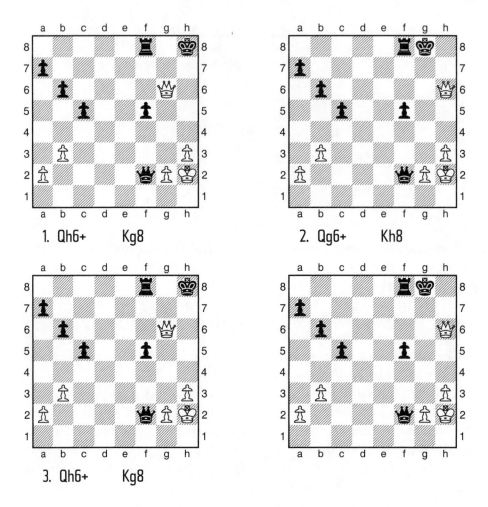

1. Qh6+   Kg8

2. Qg6+   Kh8

3. Qh6+   Kg8

Again after 4. Qxg6+ the same position will be reached for the third time.

Insufficient mating material

A game is a draw when neither player has enough material (pieces or pawns) with which to checkmate the opponent's king. In this example, each player has only a bishop, which is not enough to force checkmate. The game is a draw.

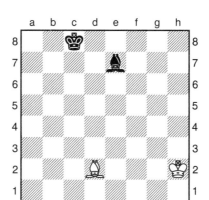

These are some examples of insufficient checkmating material:

- King versus king
- Bishop and king versus king
- Knight and king versus king
- Two knights and king versus king

The 50-move rule

If the two players make 50 moves without a capture or a pawn advance, either player can claim a draw by applying the 50-move rule. This rule was created to avoid continuing a game in which neither side can make progress.

How to Record Chess Moves

Recording the moves on a scoresheet is mandatory for both players in tournament games. The system used in this book is called algebraic notation.

The system is based on a grid. There are eight files, which are designated by the letters a to h, starting from White's left side. There are eight ranks, which are designated by the numbers 1 to 8, starting from White's first rank. Each square on the board is identified by a combination of the letter of the file followed by the number of the rank.

To record a move, first write the symbol of the piece that is being moved, then the coordinates of the square to which the piece is being moved. If the piece is a pawn, omit the symbol.

An "x" is used if the move is a capture. The symbol "+" indicates check, and the symbol "#" indicates checkmate.

Moves are recorded in two columns. The left column is for White's move, the right column for Black's moves. Here is an example of a 19-move game. After each move, compare the position on your chessboard with the diagram to make sure it is correct.

White	Black
1. e4	d5

The recorded move e4 means the pawn on the e-file moves to e4. There is no need to use the abbreviation P for a pawn move.

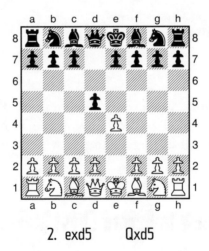

2. exd5	Qxd5

The move exd5 means the pawn on e4 captures the pawn on d5. The abbreviation of all the other pieces are used to describe the moves with two exceptions. N is used for knight and not K since that is used for the king. The name of the file is used for a pawn move, not the initial P.

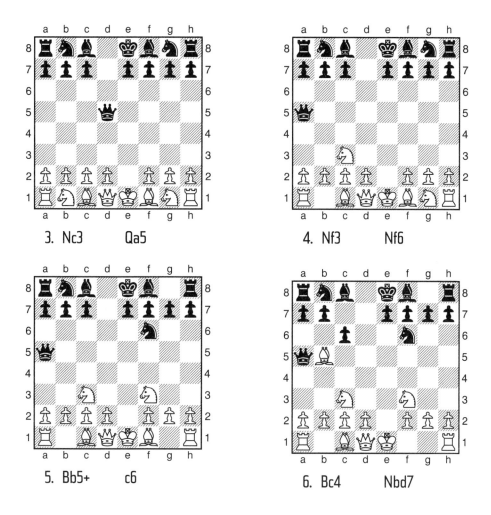

3. Nc3   Qa5

4. Nf3   Nf6

5. Bb5+   c6

6. Bc4   Nbd7

When two of the same type of piece can move to the same square, a clarification must be made to avoid confusion. Here both knights can go to d7. Therefore, a clarification is needed using the name of the file on which the moving piece stands. Nbd7 means the knight on the b-file is moving to d7.

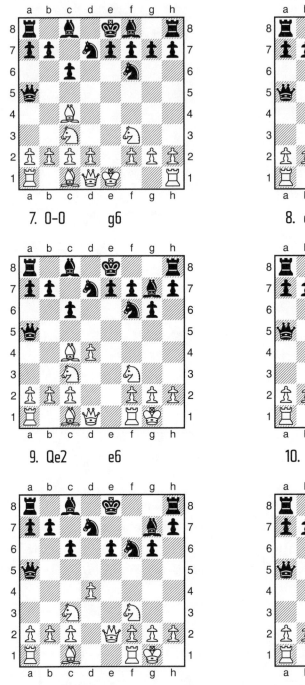

7. O-O   g6

8. d4   Bg7

9. Qe2   e6

10. Bxe6   fxe6

11. Qxe6+   Kd8

12. Ng5   Re8

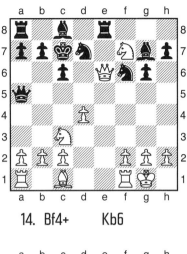

13. Nf7+   Kc7

14. Bf4+   Kb6

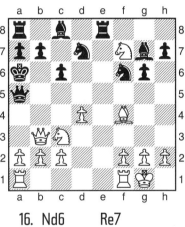

15. Qb3+   Ka6

16. Nd6   Re7

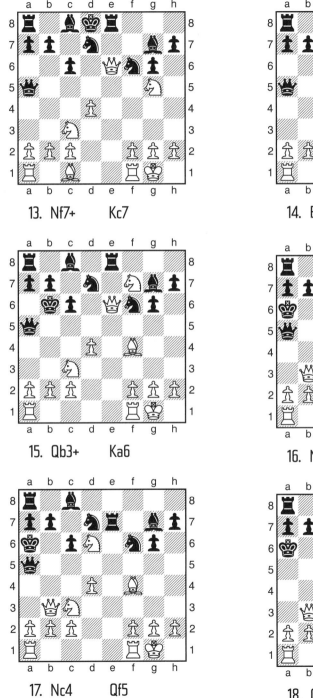

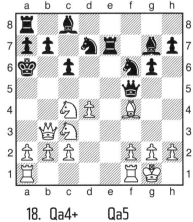

17. Nc4   Qf5

18. Qa4+   Qa5

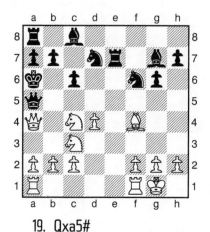

19. Qxa5#

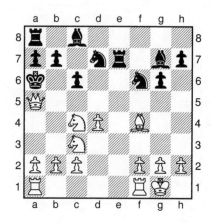

The Basic Principles of Chess

Chess is fun if it is played correctly. In order to play successfully, you should follow these very important basic principles, which are followed by players of all levels. The following are the five must-know principles of chess.

Control the center! The center is made up the four squares in the middle of the board (e4, d4, e5, and d5). The player who controls the center usually has a big advantage.

Develop your pieces as quickly as possible! Move your knights and bishops off their home squares as soon as possible. Don't bring your queen out too early. Try not to move the same piece more than once in the beginning stage of the game.

Castle as soon as possible! It is vital to keep your king safe, so castle as early as possible. Remember, you can't win if you get checkmated! After you have castled, try to connect your rooks.

Keep your pieces protected! Every piece is important. Don't leave your pieces "hanging" (undefended).

Here is the "pyramid of importance" in chess:

#1 King safety (if the king gets checkmated the game is over)

#2 Material gains (making sure you try to gain more valuable pieces than you lose)

#3 The above-mentioned strategic gains (such as center control, developing your pieces, etc.)

Have lots of fun! Win with class, lose with dignity! The most important thing in chess should be to have fun, whether you win or lose. When you win, be a good sport. When you lose, be an even better sport. Shake hands and congratulate your opponent. This will go a long way in making good friends.

Beside the five valuable principles above, there are others that you should try to remember. Chess is a game with logic, strategies, planning, and tactics. Keep the following principles in mind as you play.

Every move should have a purpose!
What is the idea behind your opponent's moves?

Always think before you move!

Learn to make plans!

Analyze your games and learn from your mistakes!
Every player, from beginner to world champion, makes mistakes. It is very important to go over your games to find mistakes and learn from them.

Pace yourself wisely!
There are many different types of time controls in chess. Use your time wisely. If you have 30, 60, or 90 minutes to play your game, use your time to find the best plans and moves. Don't rush just because your opponents play fast.

SECTION I

SECTION 1

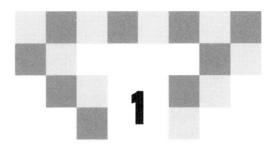

CHECKMATE IN ONE MOVE
WITH EACH OF THE PIECES

When I was growing up, my father would give me many chess puzzles to solve every day, and I really looked forward to solving them. This process helped me throughout my career and has done a lot to make me the player I am today. Now, thirty years later, I still solve chess puzzles every day, and it's also how I ask my students to practice chess on a daily basis.

In this first chapter of puzzles, you will learn the art of checkmate (often shortened to "mate") through various well-known patterns. In addition, you will learn how to checkmate in a single move with each of the different pieces.

Another thing I strongly recommend is to solve the puzzles at least three times. Make a note of how long it takes you solve each one. When you have finished all the puzzles, start over from the beginning and note your times again. You'll be amazed at how much faster you'll be the second and third times—a clear indication that practicing these patterns has helped you learn to recognize them. The more patterns you recognize, the better your chess skills will become.

It is important to try to find these solutions quickly. As your game improves, you will want to be able to see these checkmates accurately from a distance of many moves.

Try to solve these puzzles without using a board. In the beginning you may want to set up these positions on a chessboard, but as soon as you get the hang of it, solve them by looking at the book, not the board. This process will help you improve your calculation and visualization skills. These are two very critical skills in chess. Professional chess players can visualize the chessboard in their minds and some can calculate up to a few dozens moves mentally without looking at the board at all.

In order to find checkmate, you obviously need to attack the enemy king. The next thing you need to do is to make sure the king has no escape. As we learned in the tutorials, a king can escape in three possible ways: a) the king moves to a safe square; b) another piece blocks the check; c) another piece captures the attacking piece.

The solutions are at the end of the chapter.

A) Checkmate with the Queen

1. The Black king is trapped in the corner. Can you find a checkmate for White?

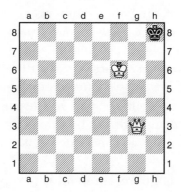

2. The Black king is trapped on the side of the board. Can you find a checkmate for White?

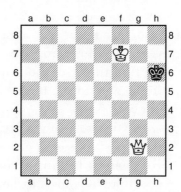

3. The Black king is trapped on the side of the board. Can you find a checkmate for White?

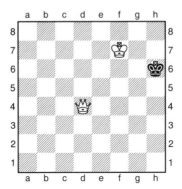

4. The Black king is trapped at the end of the board. Can you find a checkmate for White?

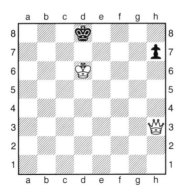

5. The Black king is trapped at the end of the board. Can you find a checkmate for White?

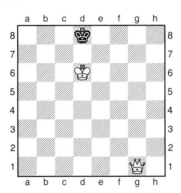

6. The Black king is trapped at the end of the board. Can you find a checkmate for White?

7. The Black king is trapped on the side of the board. Can you find a checkmate for White?

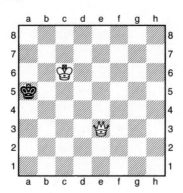

8. The Black king is trapped at the end of the board. Can you find a checkmate for White?

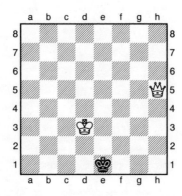

9. The Black king is trapped on the first rank. Can you find a checkmate for White?

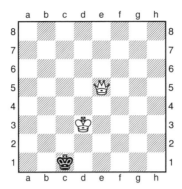

10. White is down a rook but can checkmate Black. Can you find the checkmate for White?

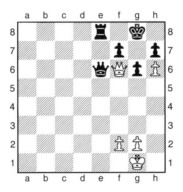

11. Black is threatening to checkmate White. Can you save White by checkmating Black first?

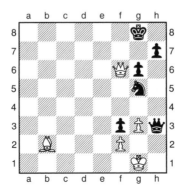

12. The Black king is stuck near the corner. Can you find the checkmate for White?

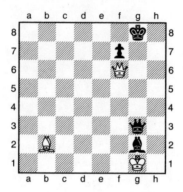

13. Black has more material but White can win. Can you find the checkmate for White?

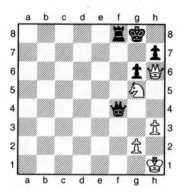

14. Black is threatening to checkmate White. Can you save White by checkmating Black first?

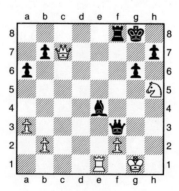

15. Black has more material but White can win. Can you find the checkmate for White?

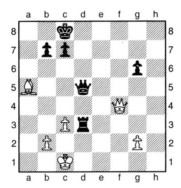

16. Black is ahead in material but White can win. Can you find the checkmate for White?

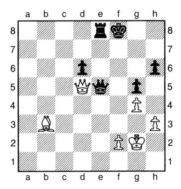

17. Black has more material but White can win. Can you find the checkmate for White?

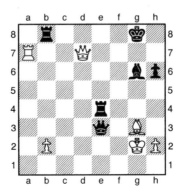

18. The two sides have even material but White can win. Can you find the checkmate for White?

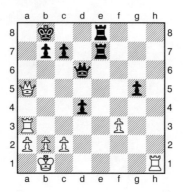

19. White has a checkmate in one move. Can you find it?

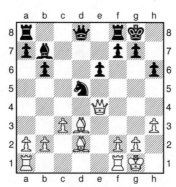

20. The two sides have even material but White can checkmate in one move. Can you find it?

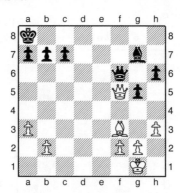

B) Checkmate with a Rook

21. Here we see how to checkmate with a rook. Can you find the checkmate in one move for White?

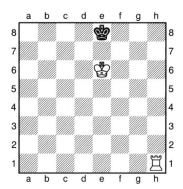

22. The Black king is stuck on the side. Can White take advantage of this and checkmate in one move?

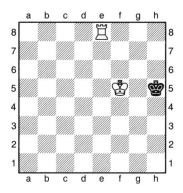

23. White can checkmate Black in one move. Can you find it?

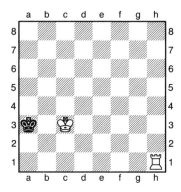

24. Both sides have equal material but White has checkmate in one move.

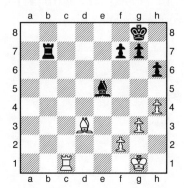

25. White has a checkmate in one move. Can you find it?

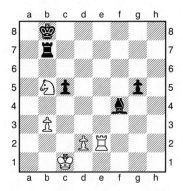

26. Black is threatening checkmate. Can White checkmate Black first?

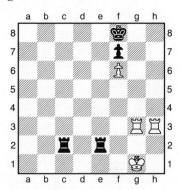

27. White can checkmate Black next move. Can you find this checkmate?

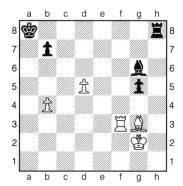

28. White has a checkmate in one move. Can you find this clever mate?

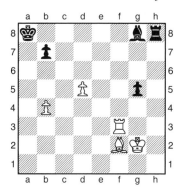

29. Black's king is isolated on the side of the board. Can you find the checkmate for White?

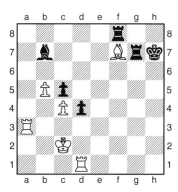

30. Black is up a pawn but White has a checkmate in one move. Can you find it?

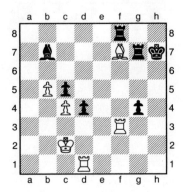

31. Black is up a pawn but White has a checkmate in one move. Can you find it?

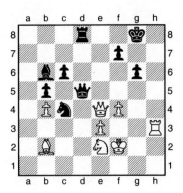

32. Both sides still have a lot of pieces but White has a checkmate in one move. Can you find it?

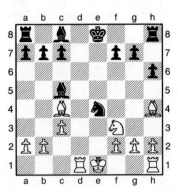

33. White has a tricky checkmate in one move. Can you find it?

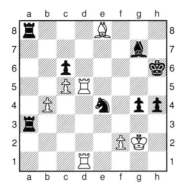

34. Black's king is stuck in the corner. Can you find the mate in one move for White?

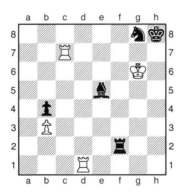

35. The White queen is under attack but White has a checkmate in one move. Where is it?

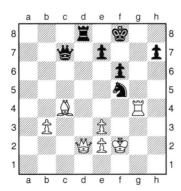

36. Black is about to promote the b-pawn but White has a checkmate. Can you find it?

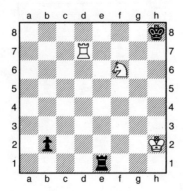

37. Black is up a rook but White has a checkmate in one move. Can you find the mate?

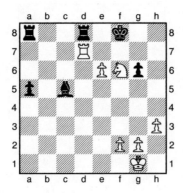

38. Can White take advantage of the exposed Black king and checkmate in one move?

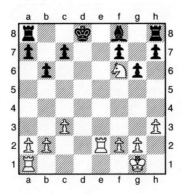

39. White has a checkmate in one move. Can you find it?

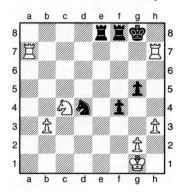

40. The two sides have equal material but White can checkmate. C
you find it?

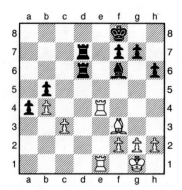

C) Checkmate with a Bishop

41. The Black king is in the corner. How can White checkmate?

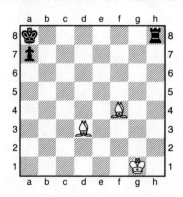

42. Black is ahead in material, but it does not help here. Why?

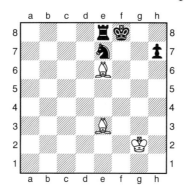

43. Black is behind in development and has not safeguarded the King. What should White play?

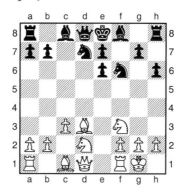

44. The Black king is in the corner. How can White checkmate?

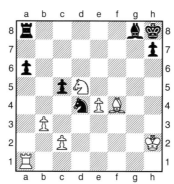

45. Black is ahead in material, but White wins anyway. How?

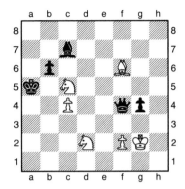

46. Black is up a pawn, but it does not help here. Why?

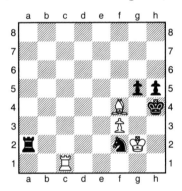

47. The Black king is in an unsafe place. Where does the danger come from?

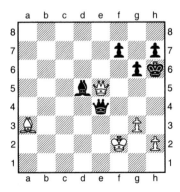

48. The Black king is in enemy territory. How can White checkmate?

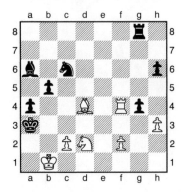

49. Black seems to be doing well, but White has prepared a surprise. Where?

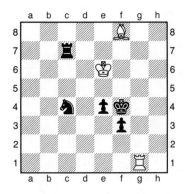

50. The position looks quite even, but White has a mate in one move.

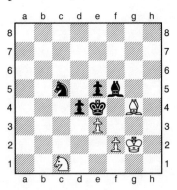

51. The position seems balanced. Can you find a checkmate in one move for White?

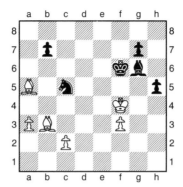

52. The Black king never managed to castle. How should White continue?

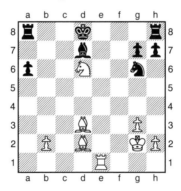

53. The Black king has no safe place to go to. So all we need to do is attack it.

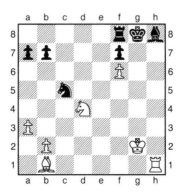

54. Black seems to be in good shape. But it is White's move and White has a mate in one move.

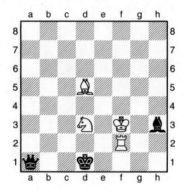

55. The Black king is cornered. How can White checkmate in one move?

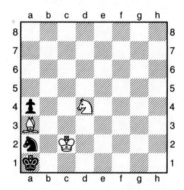

56. The Black king is under attack from all sides. Where does the final blow come from?

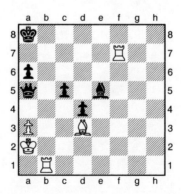

57. This time it is Black's move. How does Black checkmate White in one move?

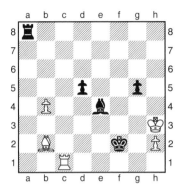

58. White's last move was h2–h3. What can Black do now? Is there a checkmate?

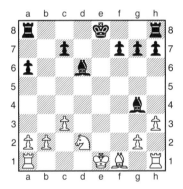

59. White is threatening to checkmate Black in one move. But it is Black's turn to checkmate.

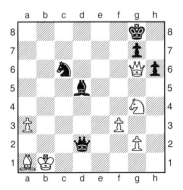

60. White threatens checkmate. But Black's checkmate comes first. Where is the mate?

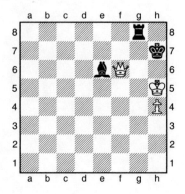

D) Checkmate with a Knight

61. White can give a smothered mate. Can you see how?

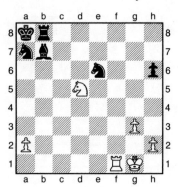

62. The Black king is stuck. White has a checkmate in one move. Can you find it?

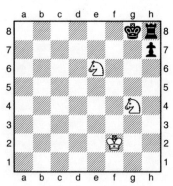

63. Here is a meeting of the knights. What should White play?

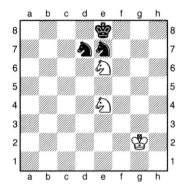

64. Black is up two pawns, but White can checkmate. How?

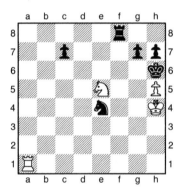

65. Black has a queen and White does not. But the Black king is in danger. Why?

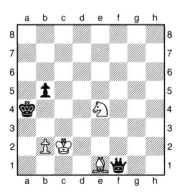

66. Black is ahead in material. How can White checkmate in one?

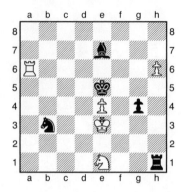

67. The White knight is under attack. Where should it go?

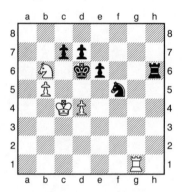

68. Again the White knight is under attack. Where should it go?

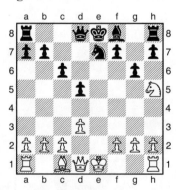

69. Black has just played 1. ... Kb5–a4, attacking White's rook on b3. What should White do?

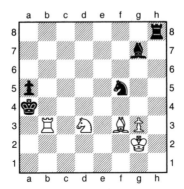

70. Here White needs the help of a "pin." Can you find the checkmate?

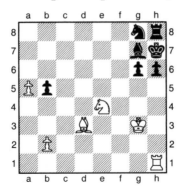

71. Here White has a strong attack on the Black king. How can White end the game?

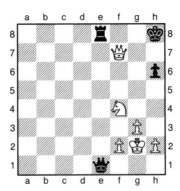

72. White to move. How can White checkmate?

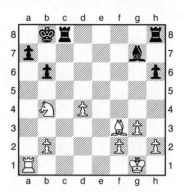

73. The Black king is in the middle with only one safe space to go to. What should White play?

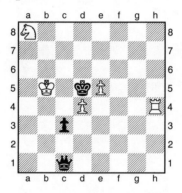

74. Black is a pawn up and played a forking move attacking White's rook and pawn. But . . .

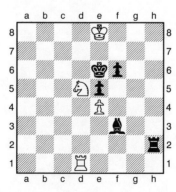

75. Is it checkmate with 1. Nxe7+ or 1. Nb6+? Or both?

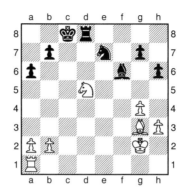

76. How can White checkmate in one move?

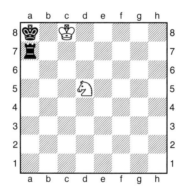

77. Black to move and checkmate in one move. How?

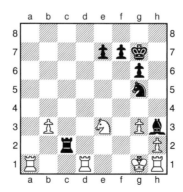

78. The White king has attacked the Black rook. Should it move away?

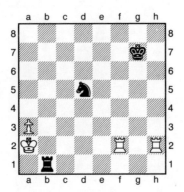

79. White is ahead in material, but Black can checkmate. How?

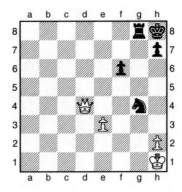

80. The White queen threatens to checkmate on g7 or h8. What can Black do?

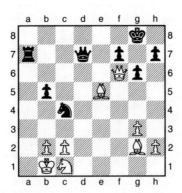

E) Checkmate with a Pawn

81. White has only one pawn left, but it's a powerful one! What is the correct move?

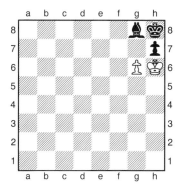

82. Black has just offered to exchange bishops. What should White do?

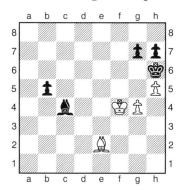

83. Black has an extra pawn. But it is White's move. What would you play?

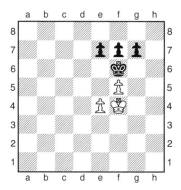

84. Black has an extra knight. How can White checkmate in one move?

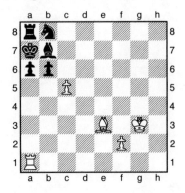

85. The Black knight is attacking the White bishop. What should White do?

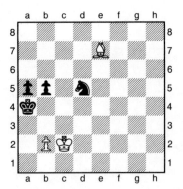

86. White can capture the Black bishop or pawn. Which is the right choice?

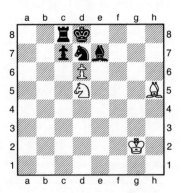

87. Black seems to be doing well. Is this true? Does White have a mate in one move?

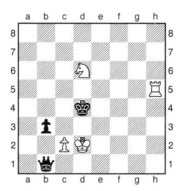

88. How can White checkmate in one move?

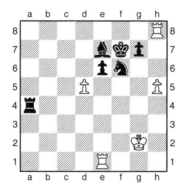

89. The White rook is under attack. What should White do?

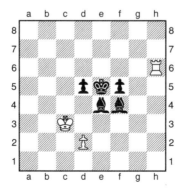

90. White can capture Black's g4 pawn with two different pawns. Which is correct?

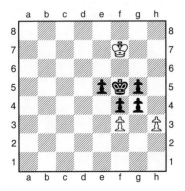

91. If it were Black's move, Black could checkmate in one move, but it is White's turn. What's the right move?

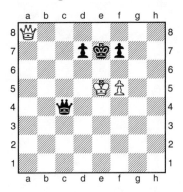

92. White can attack Black's king with two pawns. Should it be the pawn on the c-file or the e-file?

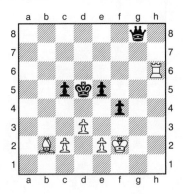

93. Black has two rooks for White's rook and bishop. But White can checkmate in one move. How?

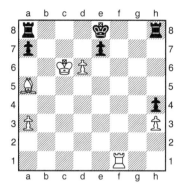

94. Which pawn should White push to checkmate?

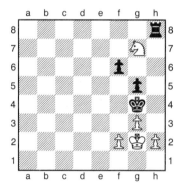

95. White's d-pawn can capture either of Black's two pawns. Does it matter which one White takes?

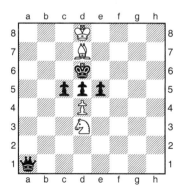

96. White can capture the pawn on a3. Is there any better move?

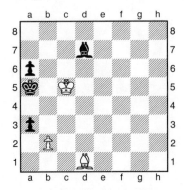

97. Black to move. How can Black checkmate?

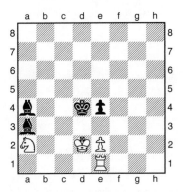

98. Black is down a pawn but doesn't mind at all. Why?

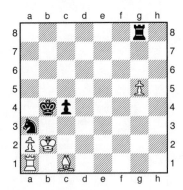

99. How can Black checkmate in one move?

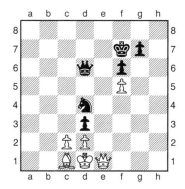

100. Black's rook and pawn are under attack. What can Black do?

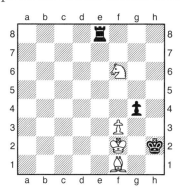

Solutions

1) 1. Qg7#.
2) 1. Qg6#.
3) 1. Qh4#.
4) 1. Qd7#.
5) 1. Qg8#.
6) 1. Qb5# (after 1. Qa1+ Ba4 blocks).
7) 1. Qa3#.
8) 1. Qe2#.
9) 1. Qa1#.
10) 1. Qg7#.
11) 1. Qg7#.
12) 1. Qh8#.
13) 1. Qxh7#.
14) 1. Qg7#.
15) 1. Qxc7#.
16) 1. Qf7#.
17) 1. Qg7#.
18) 1. Qa8#.
19) 1. Qh7#.
20) 1. Qc8#.
21) 1. Rh8#.
22) 1. Rh8#.
23) 1. Ra1#.
24) 1. Rc8#.
25) 1. Re8#.
26) 1. Rh8#.
27) 1. Ra3#.
28) 1. Rf8#.
29) 1. Rh3#.
30) 1. Rh1#.
31) 1. Rh8#.
32) 1. Rd8#.
33) 1. Rh5#.
34) 1. Rh7#.
35) 1. Rg8#.
36) 1. Rh7#.
37) 1. Rf7#.
38) 1. Re8#.
39) 1. Rag7# (the rook on the a-file moves to g7).
40) 1. Re8#.
41) 1. Be4#.
42) 1. Bh6#.
43) 1. Bg6#.
44) 1. Be5#.
45) 1. Bc3#.
46) 1. Bg3#.
47) 1. Bf8#.
48) 1. Bb2#.
49) 1. Bh6#.
50) 1. Bf3#.
51) 1. Bd8#.
52) 1. Ba5#.
53) 1. Bh7#.
54) 1. Bb3#.
55) 1. Bb2#.
56) 1. Be4#.
57) 1. ... Bf5#.
58) 1. ... Bg3#.
59) 1. ... Ba2#.
60) 1. ... Bg4#.
61) 1. Nb6#.
62) 1. Nh6#.
63) 1. Nd6#.
64) 1. Ng4#.
65) 1. Nc5#.
66) 1. Nd3#.
67) 1. Nc8#.
68) 1. Nf6#.
69) 1. Nc5#.
70) 1. Ng5# (the pawn on h6 is pinned; it can't capture because that would expose the king to check).
71) 1. Ng6#.

72) 1. Na6#.

73) 1. Nc7#.

74) 1. Nc7#.

75) Only 1. Nb6 is mate.

76) 1. Nb6#.

77) 1. ... Nf3#.

78) No, 1. ... Nc3# is better.

79) 1. ... Nf2#.

80) 1. ... Nd2#.

81) 1. g7#.

82) 1. g5#.

83) 1. e5#.

84) 1. cxb6#.

85) 1. b3#.

86) Capture the bishop: 1. dxe7#.

87) 1. c3#.

88) 1. dxe6#.

89) 1. d4#.

90) With the h-pawn: 1. hxg4#.

91) 1. f6#.

92) 1. e4 would allow Black to capture en passant. That is why only 1. c4 is mate.

93) 1. d7#.

94) 1. f3# (after 1. h3+ Rxh3 captures the pawn).

95) Yes, only 1. dxc5# works.

96) Yes, 1. b4#.

97) 1. ... e3#.

98) 1. ... c3#.

99) 1. ... dxc2#.

100) 1. ... g3#.

2

CAPTURING PIECES

This chapter will help you develop the sharp eye necessary to keep you alert to the possibility of capturing your opponents' unprotected pieces. You will also learn how to attack and capture pieces that do not have enough protection. These are very important parts of chess and it was part of the exercises that I used to do daily as I grew up. You want to train yourself to recognize the unprotected pieces in a split second. The only way to develop that skill is by solving these and similar exercises repeatedly. It is one of the basic principles of chess to keep all your pieces protected at all times. When your opponents forget this principle, make sure you're ready to take full advantage!

1. Can you find Black's unprotected piece and capture it?

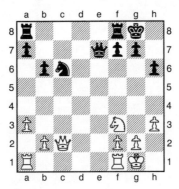

2. Does Black have any unprotected piece that White can capture? Where?

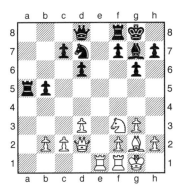

3. What can White capture?

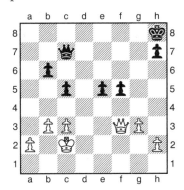

4. White can win material next move. What should White play?

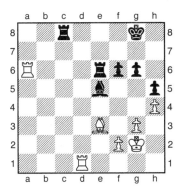

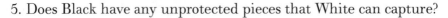

5. Does Black have any unprotected pieces that White can capture?

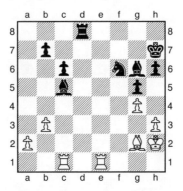

6. What piece can White capture to go ahead in material?

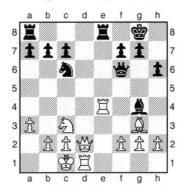

7. Is there a Black piece left unprotected that White can capture?

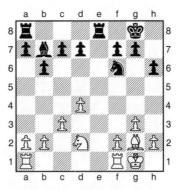

8. What is White's best move now? What can White capture?

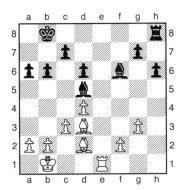

9. Is there an unprotected Black piece that White can capture?

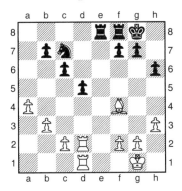

10. What is White's best move?

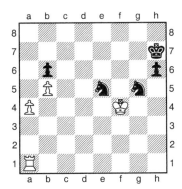

11. What is White's best move?

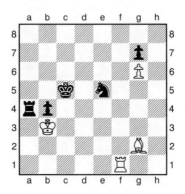

12. What should White play?

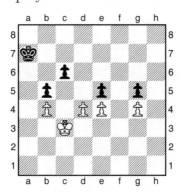

13. Black is in check. What is the best move for Black?

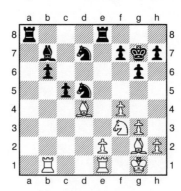

14. It is Black's turn to move. What is Black's best move?

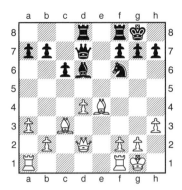

15. What is the best move for Black? What should Black capture?

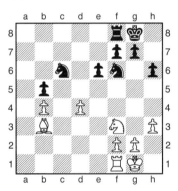

16. It is Black's turn to move. What is Black's best move?

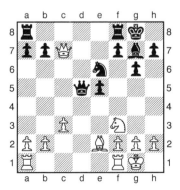

17. It is White to move. What should White do?

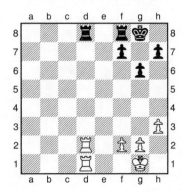

18. White is to move next. What should White play to win a piece?

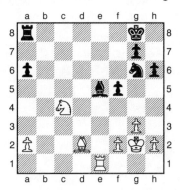

19. Black is attacking the White queen. What should White play to win material?

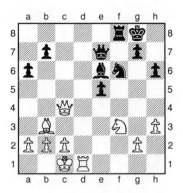

20. It is White's turn to move. Can you find the best move for White to win material?

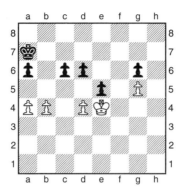

Solutions

1) The Black knight is unprotected, so 1. Qxc6.

2) Yes, the rook, so 1. Qxa5.

3) A pawn, with 1. Qxf5.

4) Capture the Black rook with 1. Rxe6.

5) Yes, a bishop. 1. Rxc5.

6) The bishop, with 1. Rxg4. But 1. Rxe8+ is only a trade of pieces, as Black can recapture with 1. ... Rxe8.

7) Yes, the Black bishop with 1. Bxb7.

8) 1. Bxa6 captures a pawn.

9) Yes, the knight, with 1. Bxc7. On the other hand, 1. Bxh6 is bad, as the g7 pawn can capture the bishop.

10) Capture the knight with 1. Kxe5.

11) 1. Kxa4 captures Black's rook.

12) Take the pawn with 1. dxe5.

13) Capture the piece that is giving the check, with 1. ... cxd4.

14) Capture the bishop with 1. ... Nxe4.

15) Capture the unprotected pawn with 1. ... Nxb4.

16) 1. ... Nxc7 captures White's queen.

17) Capture the rook with 1. Rxd8, and 1. ... Rxd8 is answered by 2. Rxd8+.

18) 1. Nxe5 (but not 1. Rxe5 Nxe5) and after 1. ... Nxe5 2. Rxe5 and White wins a bishop.

19) Capture the bishop that is attacking the queen, with 1. Qxe6+. You had to notice that the bishop on b3 is protecting the White queen on e6.

20) White wins a pawn with 1. dxe5, as 1. ... dxe5 is followed by 2. Kxe5.

GETTING OUT OF CHECK

There are three possible ways to get out of check:

1. Move your king to a square where it is not in check.
2. Put one of your pieces between your king and the piece that is checking it.
3. Capture the piece that is checking your king.

This chapter demonstrates how to get out of check using all three methods. It will be your job to determine the best way of getting out of a check in each of the puzzles. Eventually, you will develop a sense for finding best solution.

When I observe young chess players, I notice a common bad habit when it comes to checks. The player who is in check often makes the very first move that comes to mind, usually touching the king and looking where to move it without giving it much thought. It can sometimes be a very bad move that can cost the game.

You need to examine every check thoroughly. One of the things my father used to have me do is to sit on my hands while playing. That way, I could not make a move too quickly. I had to take my time and look at all my options. Sometimes my opponent's check might be a blunder and I could capture the checking piece. The lesson was that I had to take my time to look for the best response.

1. How should White get out of check?

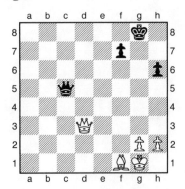

2. What is the best way for White to get out of check?

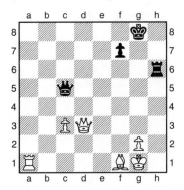

3. What is the best way for White to get out of check?

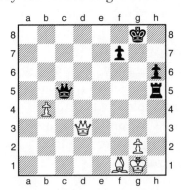

4. White has a number of ways to get out of this check. What is the best way?

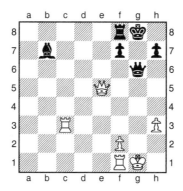

5. Black is checking White. How should White get out of check?

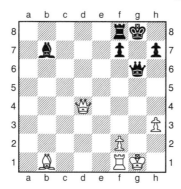

6. The Black knight is checking the White king. What should White do?

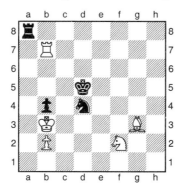

7. The Black bishop is checking the White king. What is White's response?

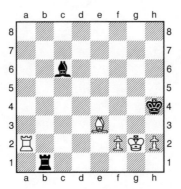

8. The Black knight is checking the White king. How should White respond?

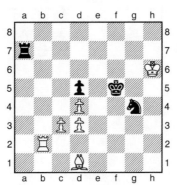

9. The Black rook is checking the White king. What should White do?

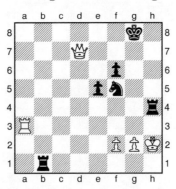

10. The Black bishop is checking the White king. How should White get out of check?

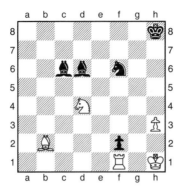

11. The Black bishop is checking the White king. What is White's best move?

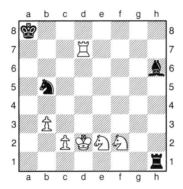

12. Black's bishop is checking the White king. White is White's best defense?

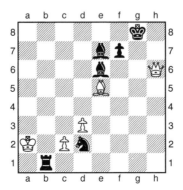

13. The White queen is checking the Black king. What is Black's best move?

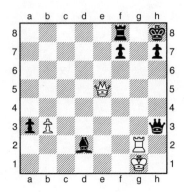

14. The Black king is in check. What is Black's best defense?

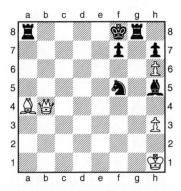

15. Black is in check. What is Black's best move?

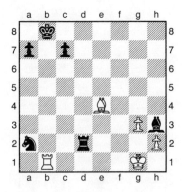

16. Black is in check. How should Black defend against the check?

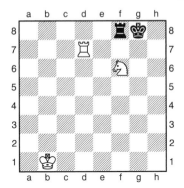

17. The White king is in check. What is White's best response?

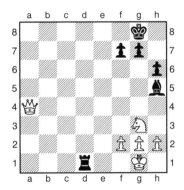

18. The Black rook is checking the White king. How should White respond?

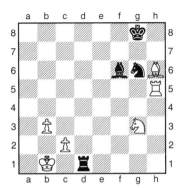

19. White is in check. Does White have a good defense?

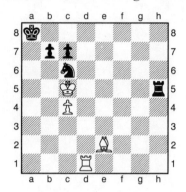

20. White is in check. What is the best way to defend?

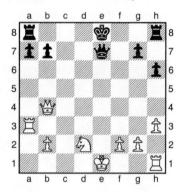

Solutions

1) Simply 1. Kh1. Blocking the check with the queen, with 1. Qd4 or 1. Qe3, is bad because Black captures the queen.

2) Now White is not able to move out of check. The only way to defend is to block it. The correct answer is 1. Qd4; now if 1. ... Qxd4+ then 2. cxd4 and each side has captured the enemy queen.

3) Here White is still not able move the king out of the check. Blocking is not a good choice either. But White can capture Black's queen with 1. bxc5.

4) Moving the king is possible, but Black checkmates after 1. Kh2 Qg2#. Blocking with the queen on g3 is okay but the best answer by far is 1. Rg3 pinning the queen. Since the queen is worth 9 points and the rook only 5 points, White would win a decisive material advantage: the Black queen.

5) Here the best choice is to capture the queen with 1. Bxg6.

6) Take Black's pawn with 1. Kxb4.

7) The only legal move here is to block the check with the pawn by 1. f3.

8) White must capture the Black knight with 1. Bxg4+. If 1. Kh5 Rh7# follows.

9) There is only one possible move: 1. Rh3.

10) The king has no escape, however, 1. Nxc6 kills the bishop.

11) Best is to move out of check with 1. Kd3. Blocking the check results in losing the knight.

12) White can capture the bishop with 1. Qxe6, but that's a bad move as 1. ... fxe6 wins the queen. Blocking with 1. c4 is the right move.

13) Black has only one move: 1. ... f6.

14) Black should block the check with 1. ... Ne7.

15) After blocking the check, Black loses a piece. Therefore, best is to play 1. ... Kc8.

16) Moving out of the check with 1. ... Kh8 is not good as White checkmates with 2. Rh7. But Black can capture the knight with 1. ... Rxf6.

17) Block the check with 1. Nf1. Then 1. ... Be2 can be answered by the fork 2. Qe8+, winning the Black bishop.

18) After the natural 1. Ka2 comes 1. ... Ra1#. Therefore 1. Bc1 is a must.

19) White can block the check with 1. Rd5, but much better is capturing Black's rook with 1. Bxh5.

20) Best is to block the check by 1. Re3 pinning Black's queen.

4

FORKS

Forks are an essential part of chess tactics. A fork is a move that uses one piece to attack two or more enemy pieces at the same time. The intention is to try to achieve a material advantage since the opponent can only counter one of the two (or more) threats.

This tactical motif is fun and also very powerful. I have always enjoyed using forks in my games and this tactic has worked many times. It's a good feeling to know that what I practiced at home could be useful in actual games.

In this chapter you will learn how to use forks with the queen, rook, bishop, knight, pawn, and king. The puzzles are harder at the end of the chapter, where you learn to set up a fork in two moves.

1. It is White's turn to move. Can you find the fork for White that wins large material?

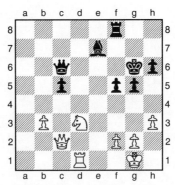

2. Black is ahead in material but White can win the queen with a fork. Can you find it?

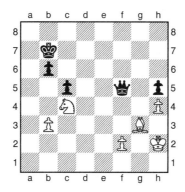

3. White, to move, has a beautiful fork. How is it done?

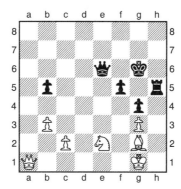

4. The two sides have equal material but White has a winning fork.

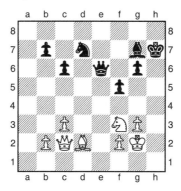

5. White, to move, has a winning fork. Can you see it?

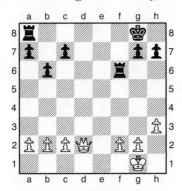

6. The game seems even, but White has a fork here. Can you find it?

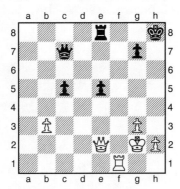

7. White has a nice fork here. Can you find it?

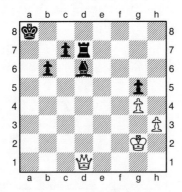

8. White, to move, has a fork. Where is it?

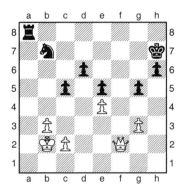

9. White, to move, can create a fork with this move. What is the right move?

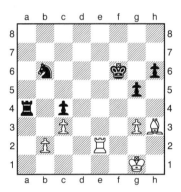

10. Unless White wins the bishop, this is a theoretical draw. How can White fork?

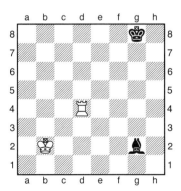

11. Black is ahead in material. Can you find a fork for White this move?

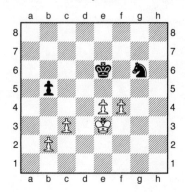

12. The two sides have equal material, but White can win with a fork. Where is it?

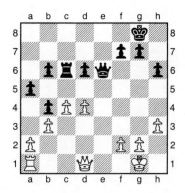

13. Black, to move, can play a fork to win. Can you find it?

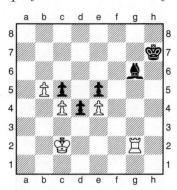

14. Black is in check but has a way to get out of check with a fork.

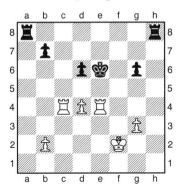

15. Black, to move, can play a fork. Where is it?

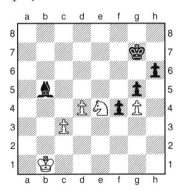

16. How can Black fork?

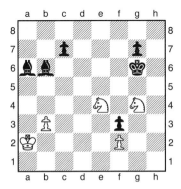

17. White, to move, can set up a forced fork in two moves. How?

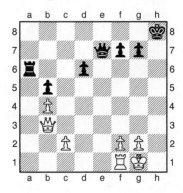

18. White, to move, has a winning fork in two moves. Where is it?

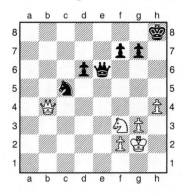

19. White, to move, has a fork in two moves. Can you find it?

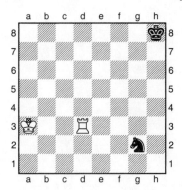

20. White can fork the Black rook in two moves. How is it done?

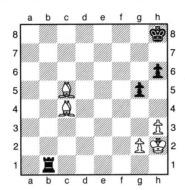

Solutions

1) 1. Ne5+ forks the Black queen and king. After the king gets out of check, White captures the queen on c6.

2) 1. Nd6+ wins the queen.

3) Here White can give a "family fork" by attacking three Black pieces at once: king, queen, and rook, with 1. Nf4+. After the Black king moves away, White should capture the Black queen.

4) 1. Ng5+ and Black loses the queen.

5) Here the queen is the forking piece. 1. Qd5+ wins the unprotected rook on a8.

6) Again Black suffers because the rook on e8 is unprotected. White plays 1. Qh5+.

7) Where is the unprotected piece? The rook on d7. Therefore, 1. Qa4+.

8) 1. Qf7+ wins the knight on b7.

9) 1. Re6+ wins the knight.

10) After 1. Rg4+ Black loses the bishop.

11) Here the pawn forks: 1. f5+.

12) 1. d5 forks the Black queen and rook.

13) 1. ... Bxe4+ wins White's rook.

14) In this rare situation, the king forks: 1. ... Kd5 attacks both White rooks at once.

15) 1. ... Bd3+ wins the White knight.

16) 1. ... Kf5 forks the two knights.

17) 1. Qh3+ forces Black to move over; then 1. ... Kg8 2. Qc8+ wins the rook.

18) 1. Qb8+ Kh7 and 2. Ng5+ wins Black's queen.

19) White needs to force the Black king to the same file as the knight: 1. Rh3+ Kg7 and now 2. Rg3+ wins the knight.

20) Here White forces the Black king onto the same diagonal as the rook: 1. Bd4+ Kh7 2.Bd3+ wins the rook.

5

MAKING PINS

A pin is a move that forces an opponent's piece to stay in place because moving it would expose the king or another more valuable piece behind it. A pin can be very dangerous, and sometimes it's hard to see a pin coming. It is an important part of your tactical arsenal. A pin can only be imposed by three different pieces: bishop, rook, or queen.

I did a lot of pin exercises growing up. I then helped my sisters with pins when they started to play chess. These exercises really helped all of us. But you need to do a lot of them to develop a strong tactical sense.

In this chapter you will learn how to make pins with all three of the pieces mentioned above. At first you will see examples of making pins in one move. At the end you will learn how to make pins in two moves. There are two types of pins. One, where the pinned piece cannot legally move away because doing so would illegally expose the king to check, and others, where moving the pinned piece results in material loss.

1. It is White's move. Can you see how White can pin the Black rook?

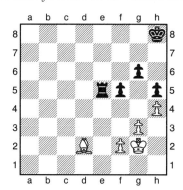

2. Look for a pin by White on the next move. Can you find it?

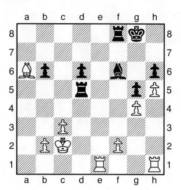

3. White can pin a Black piece this move. Can you find it?

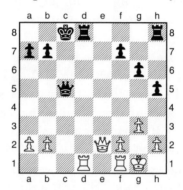

4. It is White's move and there's a very nice pin. Can you find it?

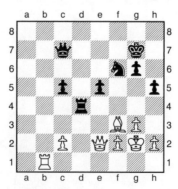

5. White can use the queen to play a pin. Can you find the winning pin?

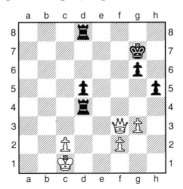

6. White can play a pin here and win a piece. Can you find it?

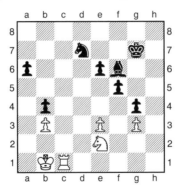

7. White, to move, can set up a devastating pin. Can you find it?

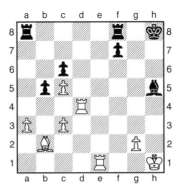

8. White can play a winning pin here. Can you find it?

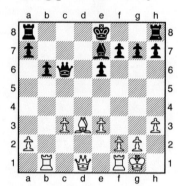

9. White is to move. Can you find a winning pin?

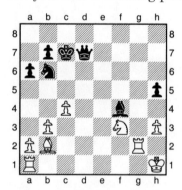

10. The two sides are equal in material, but White has a strong pin here. Can you find it?

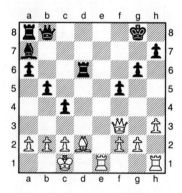

11. White to move can play a pin. Where is it?

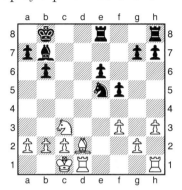

12. It is White's move. Can White play a pin?

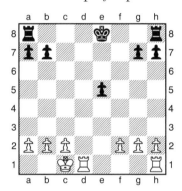

13. It is Black's move. How can Black win material with a pin?

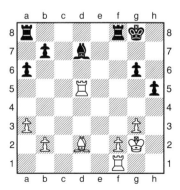

14. Material is equal, but Black can play a great pin here. How?

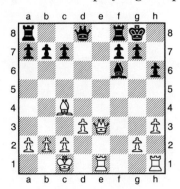

15. Black, to move, can play a very strong pin. Can you find it?

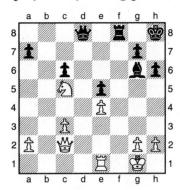

16. Black to move. Can you find a pinning move for Black?

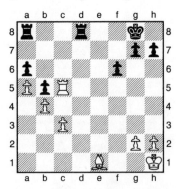

17. White to move. Can you set up a pin in two moves?

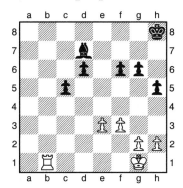

18. White is looking to set up a winning pin in two moves. Can you find it?

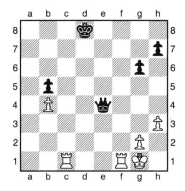

19. It is White's move. Can you set up a pin in two moves?

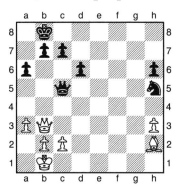

20. White to move. Can you set up a pin in two moves?

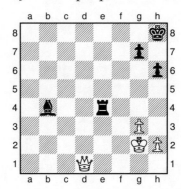

Solutions

1) 1. Bc3 and the rook cannot run away.

2) Again the Black King and rook are on the same diagonal and that's the problem: 1. Bc4.

3) 1. Rc1. It is important to note that the rook needs to be protected on c1; otherwise the queen could simply capture it.

4) 1. Rb7 is possible because the bishop on f3 defends the rook.

5) 1. Qc3 and Black can neither move the rook on d4 nor protect it.

6) White wins the knight by attacking it with 1. Rc7.

7) 1. Rh4 wins the bishop.

8) 1. Bb5 pins and wins the Black queen.

9) 1. Rg7, and the best Black can do is get a rook for the lost queen.

10) 1. Bf4. This is a relative pin. Here Black may move the rook away, but that would result in even more loss of material.

11) 1. Bf4 and the Black knight is helpless.

12) Here there are two ways to pin and win a pawn. Either rook can go to e1, but it is better to play 1. Rhe1 so the other rook can remain on the "open" d-file (open files are files that have no pawns on them).

13) Attack the rook with 1. ... Bc6.

14) 1. ... Bg5 is the move.

15) Black has to attack the White knight with 1. ... Qb6.

16) Attack the bishop: 1. ... Rd1.

17) White needs to force the Black king onto the same rank as the bishop: 1. Rb8+ Kg7 and now 2. Rb7 pins.

18) 1. Rfd1+ Ke7 and 2. Re1 wins the queen. On the other hand, 1. Rcd1+ does not work because the Black king is not forced to move to the e-file but instead will move to the c-file.

19) White chases the Black king on the same diagonal as the Black queen. 1. Qg8+ Ka7 and 2. Bg1 pins the queen.

20) Again, we need to push the Black king onto the same diagonal as the rook: 1. Qd8+ Kh7 2. Qd3.

6

USING PINS

In the previous chapter you learned how to make pins. In this chapter you will learn how to use them to your advantage. This will work very well with the knowledge you gained in the last chapter.

At first you will learn how to take advantage of existing pins to win material or even checkmate your opponent. At the end you will learn how to recognize pinned pieces and then attack them.

1. White to move. Can you take advantage of the existing pin?

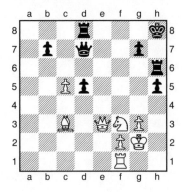

2. White to move. Can you exploit the existing pin to win material?

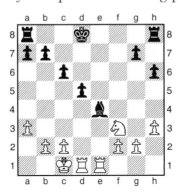

3. White to move. Is it possible for White to take advantage of the existing pin?

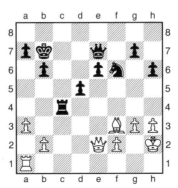

4. White to move. Can White win material using an existing pin?

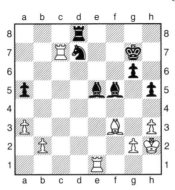

5. White to move. Can you set up a winning attack against the pinned piece?

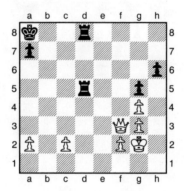

6. White to move. Is it possible to attack the pinned piece?

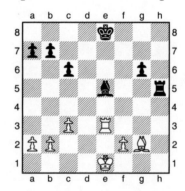

7. White to move. How can White attack the pinned piece?

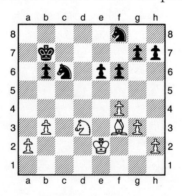

Using Pins

8. White to move. Is there a way to attack Black's pinned piece?

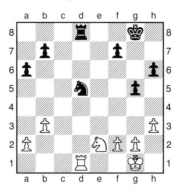

9. White to move. White has a devastating move using an existing pin. What is it?

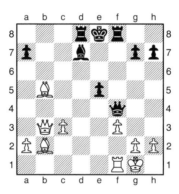

10. White to move. Can you exploit the pin and come up with a decisive move?

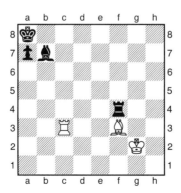

11. White to move. How can White win using an existing pin?

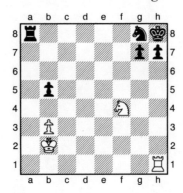

12. White to move. How can White checkmate in one move by exploiting an existing pin?

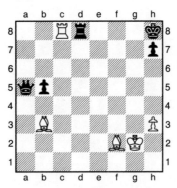

13. Black to move. Black has a crushing move using an existing pin. Can you find it?

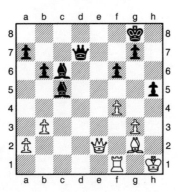

14. Black to move. Do you see how Black can take advantage of the current pin?

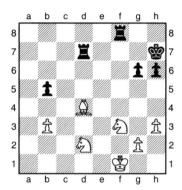

15. Black to move. Can you see how to attack the pinned piece?

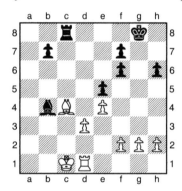

16. Black to move. Can you find a way to win by exploiting the pinned piece?

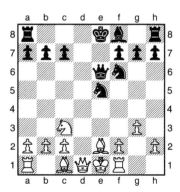

17. White to move. How can White win a knight in two moves by creating a pin?

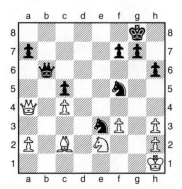

18. White to move. Can you find a way to force Black into a pin to win material in two moves?

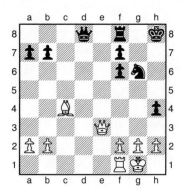

19. White to move. Can White trap a Black knight in two moves by creating a pin?

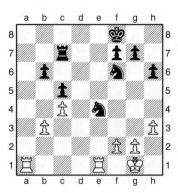

20. White to move. How can White trap the knight in two moves by creating a pin?

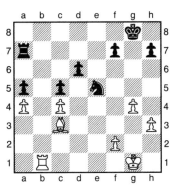

Solutions

1) Thanks to the existing pin on the g7 pawn, White can capture the rook with 1. Qxh6+.

2) White can win a bishop with 1. Rxe4.

3) Yes, White wins a rook after 1. Qxc4.

4) The knight on d7 is pinned. White wins a bishop with 1. Rxe5.

5) Yes, by attacking the rook with 1. c4.

6) Yes. Attack the bishop with 1. f4.

7) After 1. Nb4, Black's knight on c6 is lost.

8) After 1. Nc3, if Black takes with 1. ... Nxc3, Black loses the exchange (rook for knight) after 2. Rxd8+.

9) Checkmate with 1. Qe6.

10) Yes, 1. Rc8 checkmate.

11) 1. Ng6 smothered mate!

12) 1. Bd4 checkmates.

13) 1. ... Qh3#.

14) Black can capture the bishop with 1. ... Rxd4.

15) Attack the bishop with 1. ... b5.

16) Checkmate with 1. ... Nf3.

17) First force the Black king into the pin by 1. Qe8+ Kh7 and then 2. Qxe3.

18) Again, 1. Qh6+ Kg8, and now the king is in the pin, so 2. Qxg6+ works.

19) Yes, chase the Black king to the e-file with 1. Ra8+ Ke7 and use the freshly created pin by 2. f3.

20) 1. Rb8+ Kg7 and 2. f4 wins the knight.

7

SKEWERS

A skewer is an attack on a piece that forces it to move to avoid being captured, thus exposing another piece to capture by the attacker. This geometric motif may occur when two pieces are on the same rank, file, or diagonal.

The skewer is a very important tactical motif that many new chess players may have a hard time noticing. That is why I did extra skewer exercises when I started out in chess. Eventually it became a useful part of my tactical armory.

In the beginning of this chapter you will learn simple one-move skewer tactics. Toward the end, you will learn how to force your opponent into a skewer.

1. White to move. White can use a skewer to win the Black queen. Can you find it?

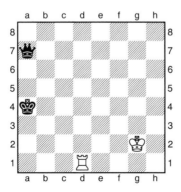

2. White to move. What is the best move for White?

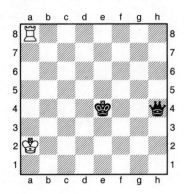

3. White to move. What is White's winning move?

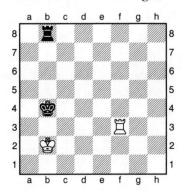

4. White to move. Can you find the best move for White?

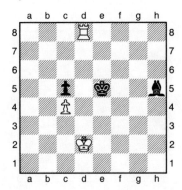

5. White to move. One correct move can win the game. Can you find it?

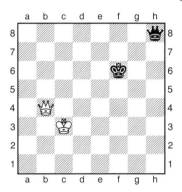

6. White to move. What is White's best move?

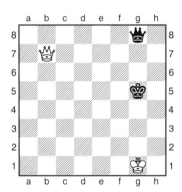

7. White to move. What should White play?

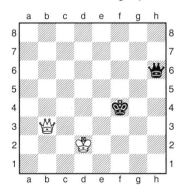

8. White to move. A proper skewer can win the game. Can you find it?

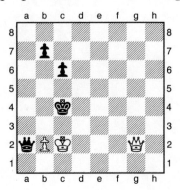

9. White to move. Black is ahead in material but White can win. Do you see how?

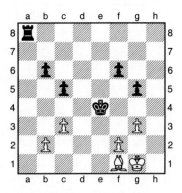

10. White to move. Can you find the best move for White?

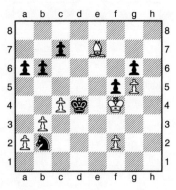

11. White to move. A proper skewer can win material. What is the right move?

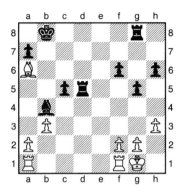

12. White to move. The correct move can win. What is it?

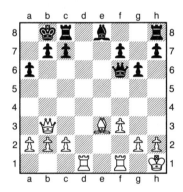

13. Black to move. Can you find the winning move?

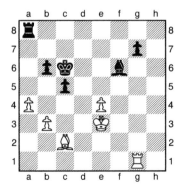

14. Black to move. How can Black win White's rook?

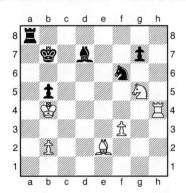

15. Black to move. One move can win. What is the right move?

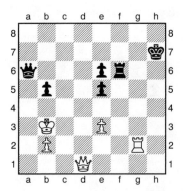

16. Black to move. What is the best move for Black?

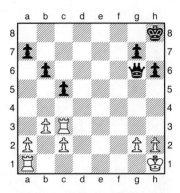

17. White to move. White can set up a game-winning skewer in two moves. How?

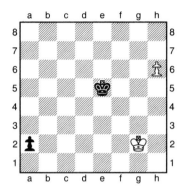

18. White to move. White can set up a winning skewer in two moves. Can you find out how?

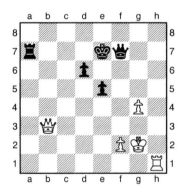

19. White to move. White is behind in material but can win a rook in two moves. How can this happen?

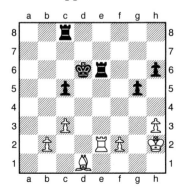

20. White to move. A two-move skewer wins for White. Can you find it?

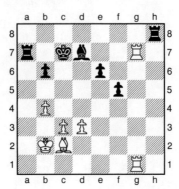

Solutions

1) 1. Ra1+. After the Black king moves, White captures the queen on a7.

2) 1. Ra4+ wins Black's queen.

3) White wins the Black rook with 1. Rb3+.

4) 1. Rd5+ wins the bishop.

5) White wins the Black queen with 1. Qd4+.

6) After 1. Qg2+, Black loses the queen.

7) Again, White takes advantage of the fact Black's king and queen are on the same diagonal: 1. Qe3+.

8) 1. Qg8+, and after the Black king moves, White captures the Black queen.

9) White can win the rook on a8 with 1. Bg2+.

10) 1. Bf6+ wins the knight.

11) After 1. Bc4, Black will lose material.

12) 1. Bd4 attacking the queen. After the queen moves, the rook on h8 is in danger.

13) Black wins a rook with 1. ... Bd4+.

14) 1. ... Ra4+.

15) 1. ... Qa4+ wins the queen on d1.

16) After the quiet 1. ... Qf6, Black wins one of the rooks.

17) Black is about to promote his pawn, so White must do the same. 1. h7 a1=Q 2. h8=Q+, and Black's new queen is lost.

18) White first trades queens with 1. Qxf7+ Kxf7 and then 2. Rh7+ wins a rook.

19) White exchanges rooks with 1. Rxe6+ Kxe6 and then 2. Bg4+ wins the rook.

20) Here White sacrifices an exchange to win material: 1. Rxd7+ Kxd7 2. Rg7+.

8

DISCOVERED ATTACKS

A discovered attack occurs when a piece moves to uncover an attack by a piece behind it. This is a very powerful tactic, allowing two pieces to attack at the same time. The most common discovered attack involves a check or a capture. It often leads either to winning material or sometimes even checkmate.

The discovered attack can be very dangerous because it is usually impossible for the opponent to defend against two simultaneous attacks. Besides, it is often easy to overlook, which is why I always recommend that my students spend extra time doing these exercises, just as I did at a young age.

In the beginning of the chapter you will learn various forms of discovered attacks in one move. The later exercises will show you how to force your opponent into a discovered attack in two moves.

1. White to move. White can win the queen with a discovered check. Can you find it?

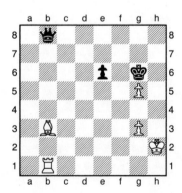

2. White to move. Look for a devastating discovered attack.

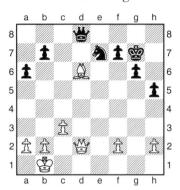

3. White to move. Black is threatening to checkmate White. What should White do?

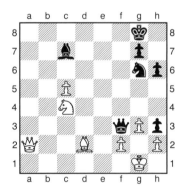

4. White to move. White can win the Black queen with a discovered check.

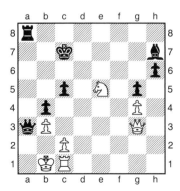

5. White to move. Can you find the best move for White?

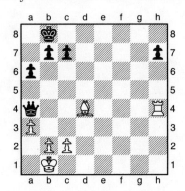

6. White to move. Can White win the Black queen?

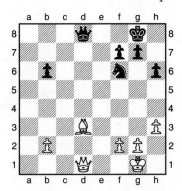

7. White to move. Black is ahead in material but White can win the queen. Do you see how?

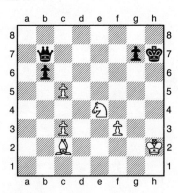

8. White to move. Can you find a way for White to win the Black queen?

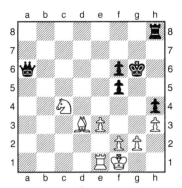

9. White to move. Black is ahead in material but White has a powerful move. What is it?

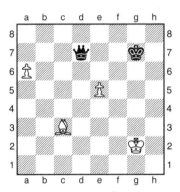

10. White to move. White is behind in material but can turn the tide and win.

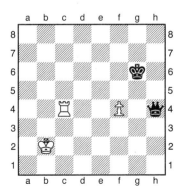

11. White to move. Material is even, but White has a winning move. Which move is it?

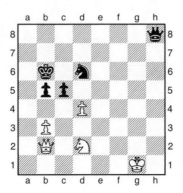

12. White to move. The game seems like a draw but it isn't. Can you find the win for White?

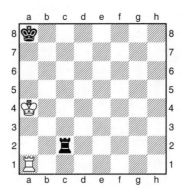

13. Black to move. Can you find a winning discovered check for Black?

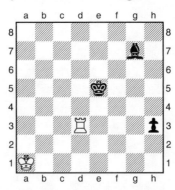

14. Black to move. How should Black proceed to win the game?

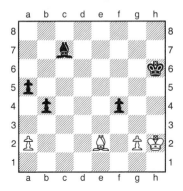

15. Black to move. Can you find the winning discovered check?

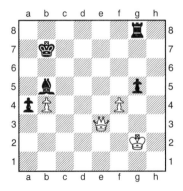

16. Black to move. Black has a winning move coming up. Can you find it?

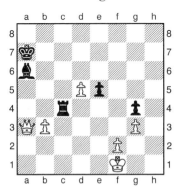

17. White to move. Can you find a two-move discovered check to win Black's rook?

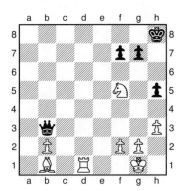

18. White to move. White can set up a winning discovered check in two moves. How?

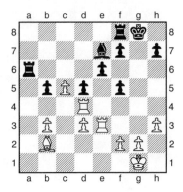

19. White to move. White has a brilliant two-move discovered check. Can you find it?

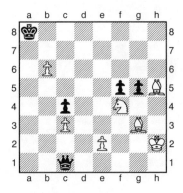

20. White to move. How can White set up a winning two-move discovered check?

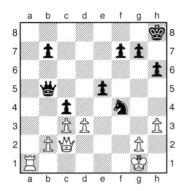

Solutions

1) 1. Bc2+, and after the king moves out of check, White captures the queen.
2) 1. Be5+ wins the queen.
3) White plays a discovered check and attacks Black's queen at the same time: 1. Ne5+.
4) 1. Nc4+ wins the Black queen.
5) White sacrifices the bishop to win the Black queen: 1. Ba7+.
6) Yes, again by sacrificing the bishop: 1. Bh7+.
7) 1. Nd6+ and Black cannot save the queen.
8) By sacrificing the knight with 1. Ne5+.
9) 1. e6+ wins the queen.
10) By giving up the last pawn: 1. f5+.
11) Capture with 1. dxc5+.
12) 1. Kb3+ wins the rook.
13) 1. ... Ke4+ and White loses the rook.
14) Discovered check with 1. ... f3+.
15) 1. ... gxf4+ and the White queen is lost.
16) 1. ... Ra4+ wins the queen. The rook cannot be captured.
17) 1. Rg3+ Kh8 sets up the discovery 2. Ra4+ and wins.
18) Forcing the king to the bishop's diagonal with 1. Rd8+ Kh7 and now 2. Nd4+.
19) 1. Bf3+ Kb8 and 2. Nd3+ wins the Black queen.
20) 1. Ra8+ Kh7 2. dxc4+ and the Black queen cannot be saved.

9

DOUBLE CHECK

A double check, a kind of discovered check, places the enemy king in check by two pieces at the same time. This is a very lethal tactical motif because there is no way to block it. A player in double check is unable to block both checks at the same time or capture both checking pieces. The only possibility is to move the king. In some cases even that is not possible, which means checkmate.

When I started out in chess I thought double check was a great weapon. I always wanted to do more and more double check puzzles. All the work you put in, even though it's tough, eventually pays off.

Below are some examples of double check. Some are checkmate in one move and some win material. Toward the end of the chapter, you will also learn how to use double check to set up checkmate in two moves.

1. White to move. Can you find a checkmate by double check in one move?

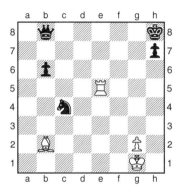

2. White to move. White has a checkmate by double check in one move. Can you find it?

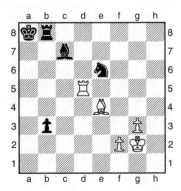

3. White to move. What is White's checkmating move?

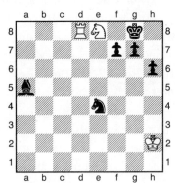

4. White to move. Can you find checkmate in the next move?

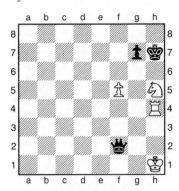

5. White to move. What is White's checkmating move?

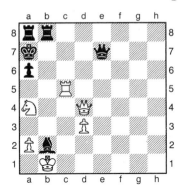

6. White to move. How can White checkmate with a double check?

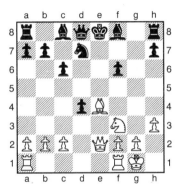

7. White to move. Can you find the unusual and lethal double check?

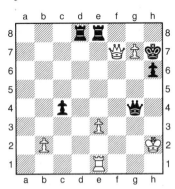

8. White to move. Can you find White's checkmating move?

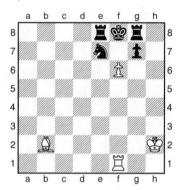

9. White to move. Can you find a double check that wins a rook for White?

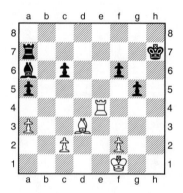

10. White to move. Can you find a double check that wins the queen?

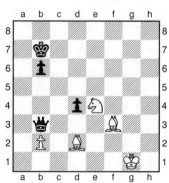

11. White to move. Does White have a double check that wins the queen?

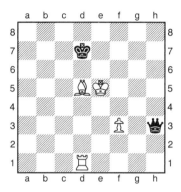

12. White to move. Can you find the double check that wins a rook?

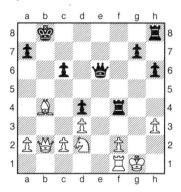

13. Black to move. Can you find the devastating double check?

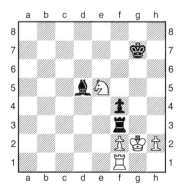

14. Black to move. Where is the double check that ends the game?

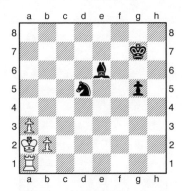

15. Black to move. One move is a double check that wins the queen.

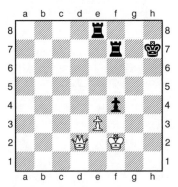

16. Black to move. Can you find the double check that wins the queen?

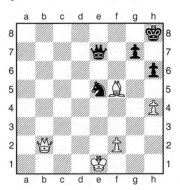

17. White to move. Can you find checkmate in two moves using a double check?

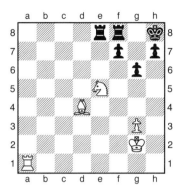

18. White to move. Can you find a checkmate in two moves using a double check?

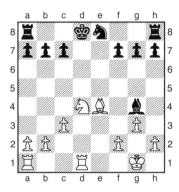

19. White to move. Where is the checkmate in two moves using a double check?

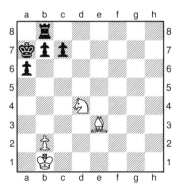

20. White to move. Find a checkmate in two moves using a double check.

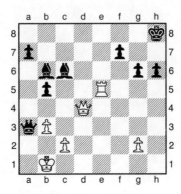

Solutions

1) 1. Re8#. The beauty is that even thought both the White bishop and rook are under attack, neither can be captured.

2) 1. Ra5# by double check.

3) The White rook is under attack, but it doesn't matter after 1. Nf6#.

4) 1. Nf6#.

5) White's queen is under attack, but that doesn't stop White from checkmating by double check with 1. Rc7#.

6) 1. Bg6#.

7) Here the solution is to promote the pawn with 1. g8=Q#.

8) There are two tries but only one works. After 1. fxe7+ Black can recapture with 1. … Kxe7. But after 1. fxg7# the game is over.

9) There are two ways to give double check. 1. Rh4+ does not achieve much after 1. … Kg8. The correct move is 1. Re7+ winning Black's rook.

10) 1. Nc5+ wins the Black queen.

11) Yes, 1. Be6+.

12) 1. Bd6+ wins the rook on f4.

13) 1. … Rg3#.

14) 1. … Nc3#. But 1. … Nb4+ is a mistake, as the White king escapes through b1.

15) 1. … fxe3+ and White loses the queen.

16) 1. … Nd3+!. The discovered check 1. … Nc4+ seems at first to be just as good, but then the White queen escapes by 2. Qe2.

17) Double check by 1. Nxf7+ Kg8 followed by 2. Nh6#.

18) 1. Nc6+ Kc8 2.Rd8#. But 1. Ne6+ does not get there, as Black has a better choice by playing 1. … Ke7.

19) 1. Nb5+ forcing 1. … Ka8 and now 2. Nxc7#.

20) 1. Re8+ Kh7 and 2. Rh8# or 2. Qh8#.

10

TRAPPING PIECES

In this chapter you will learn the art of trapping your opponents' pieces. One of the most important things you can do to help win games is to gain a material advantage. If you have more pieces than your opponent, you have a much greater chance of winning. So it is important to learn how to take advantage of your opponents' mistakes and trap their pieces.

In Chapter 2, you learned to recognize and capture "hanging" (unprotected) pieces. This chapter is a little more difficult and sophisticated. Here you will learn to recognize pieces that are in trouble and how to catch them. This skill, once mastered, will give you a real edge over your opponents, and it works even for advanced players. Besides, trapping pieces is fun!

In the beginning of this chapter you will learn to find traps in one move. Toward the end, the problems will be more difficult and you will have to find traps in two moves.

1. White to move. How can White trap the Black queen?

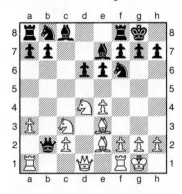

2. White to move. The objective is to trap the Black queen in one move.

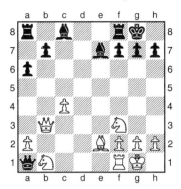

3. White to move. Can you find the one move that traps the Black queen?

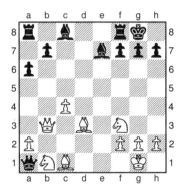

4. White to move. Look for the move that traps the Black rook.

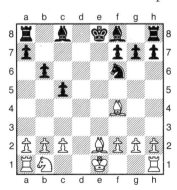

5. White to move. How can White trap the Black rook?

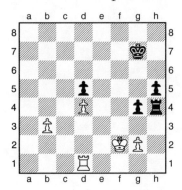

6. White to move. White can trap one of the Black rooks with this move. Can you find it?

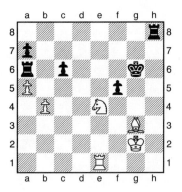

7. White to move. Is there a way to trap the Black bishop?

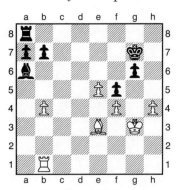

8. White to move. Is it possible to trap the queen?

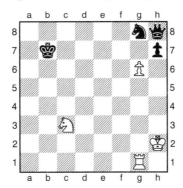

9. White to move. How can White trap the knight?

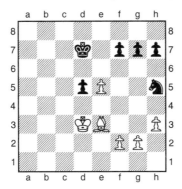

10. White to move. White can trap a Black piece. Can you see how?

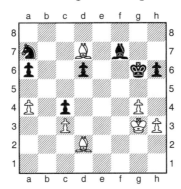

11. White to move. Look for a way to trap a Black piece.

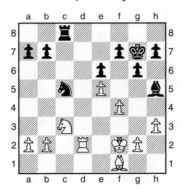

12. White to move. Can White trap any of Black's pieces?

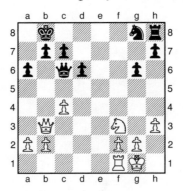

13. Black to move. What piece can Black trap and how?

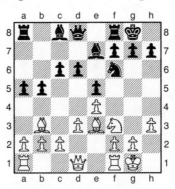

14. Black can trap one of White's major pieces. Can you see how?

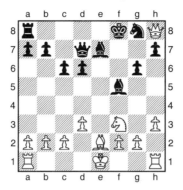

15. Black to move. White's rook is stuck. How can Black win it?

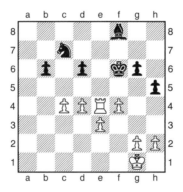

16. Black to move. What should Black play to trap a White piece?

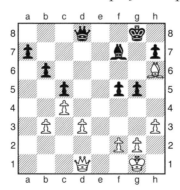

17. White to move. How can White trap the Black bishop in two moves?

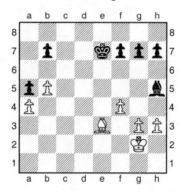

18. White to move. This one is tricky. White can trap the Black rook in two moves.

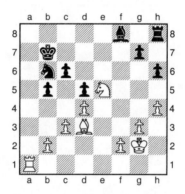

19. White to move. Do you see how White traps the Black knight in two moves?

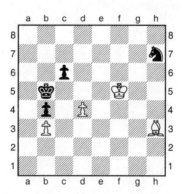

20. White to move. White can trap the Black queen in two moves. Do you see how?

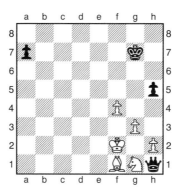

Solutions

1) The Black queen is surrounded by too many enemy pieces. 1. Na4 wins the queen.

2) The Black queen is cornered. After 1. Nc3 the queen has no safe square.

3) Again, the Black queen is in the corner. 1. Bb2 traps it.

4) White's bishop is posted nicely on the b8-h2 diagonal, and after 1. Bf3 the Black rook on a8 has no safe place to go.

5) The rook is lost after 1. Kg3.

6) 1. Nc5 wins the rook.

7) 1. b5 wins the bishop.

8) Pushing the pawn by 1. g7 takes away all the queen's escape squares.

9) A classic example of why it is not good to put a knight on the edge of the board. 1. g4 wins it.

10) Again, the Black knight is misplaced. 1. Be3 wins the knight.

11) The Black bishop has no safe square to run to after 1. g4.

12) Black pays for lagging behind in development. 1. Qc3 traps the rook on h8. The only way Black can save its rook is by giving up the knight instead on f6.

13) The White bishop on b3, by 1. ... a4.

14) The White queen is in the corner and is trapped 1. ... Bf6.

15) By attacking it with the king: 1. ... Kf5.

16) 1. ... Qf6 wins the bishop.

17) By attacking it first with 1. g4, after which the bishop's only escape is 1. ... Bg6, and then by attacking it a second time with 2. f5.

18) Black failed to completely develop his pieces. White takes advantage of this with 1. Nf7 Rg8 and then 2. Bh7 traps the rook.

19) By chasing it with 1. Kg6 Nf8 2. Kg7.

20) A queen in the corner is always suspect. 1. Bg2 Qxh2 2. Nf3.

THE BACK RANK

One of the most common mistakes that novices make is to allow back-rank checkmates. This occurs when the Black king is checkmated on the eighth rank or the White king on the first rank. It can also occur on the a-file or h-file, in which case it is called a corridor mate.

For a back-rank mate to work, the king cannot escape because it is trapped by the edge of the board. This also applies to positions where a king is mated on the a- or h-file.

In this chapter you will learn to develop the sharp eye needed to recognize the back-rank mate. In the beginning of the chapter the problems are easier, but toward the end the examples are more difficult and can take up to three moves to solve.

1. White to move. How can White checkmate on the back rank?

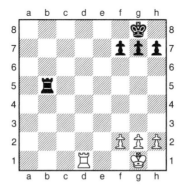

2. White to move. Look for a back-rank mate.

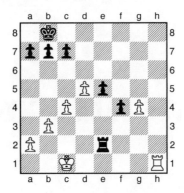

3. White to move. Is there a back-rank mate for White?

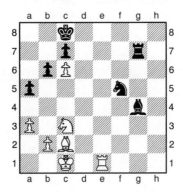

4. White to move. Even with so many pieces on the board, a back-rank mate is possible.

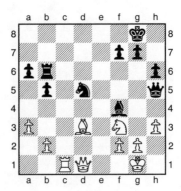

5. White to move. Is there a back-rank checkmate for White?

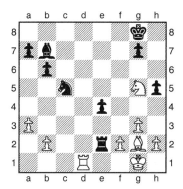

6. White to move. Can you find the back-rank mate?

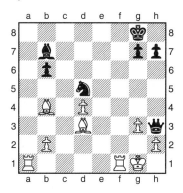

7. White to move. White is behind in material but has a back-rank mate. What is the correct move?

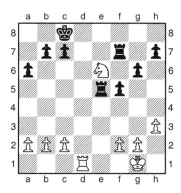

8. White to move. Find the back-rank mate.

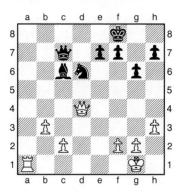

9. Black to move. The White king is trapped on the edge. What can Black do?

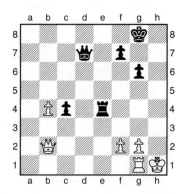

10. Black to move. Can you find the back-rank mate?

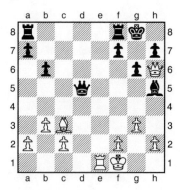

11. Black to move. Does Black have a back-rank mate?

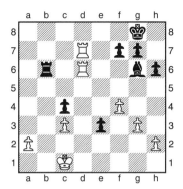

12. Black to move. Is there a back-rank mate for Black somewhere?

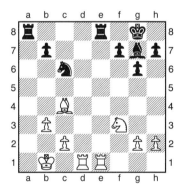

13. White to move and checkmate Black in two moves. Take advantage of the weak back rank.

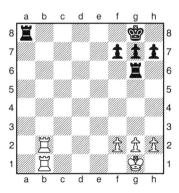

14. White to move and checkmate in two moves. Look for the back-rank mate.

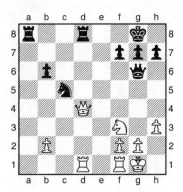

15. White to move and mate in two moves. How can White do it?

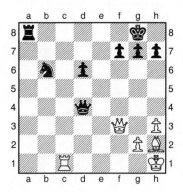

16. White to move and mate in two moves. Can you find the back-rank mate?

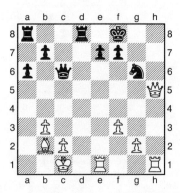

17. White to move and mate in three moves.

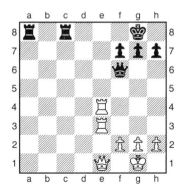

18. White to move and checkmate in three moves. Look for a mate on the side.

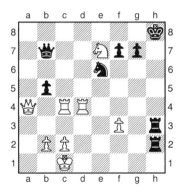

19. White to move and mate in three moves. Can you find the back-rank checkmate?

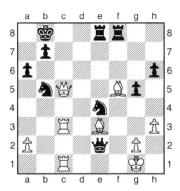

20. White to move and mate in three moves. White is looking for a back-rank mate.

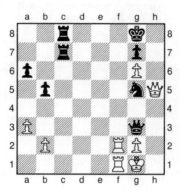

Solutions

1) 1. Rd8#. The Black king cannot escape because of its own pawns and the edge of the board.

2) 1. Rh8#, as in the previous example.

3) 1. Re8#. Here the c6 pawn aids in preventing the Black king's escape.

4) Here Black gave the king some "air" by pushing the h7 pawn to h6. But White's light-squared bishop still controls the h7 square. Therefore 1. Rc8 is mate.

5) In this position the White knight on g5 is of great help by attacking the f7 and h7 squares. 1. Rd8 is mate.

6) 1. Rf8# is possible because the bishop on b4 protects the rook.

7) Here the rook uses the knight's protection: 1. Rd8#.

8) 1. Qh8#.

9) The same mate, but this time on the side: 1. ... Rh4#.

10) Black has a knife at his neck, as White threatens mate in one move with 1. Qg7#. But Black comes first: 1. ... Qh1#.

11) Yes, with 1. ... Rb1#.

12) Yes, with 1. ... Ra1#.

13) 1. Rb8+ Rxb8 and 2. Rxb8#.

14) Now White sacrifices the queen with 1. Qxd8+ Rxd8 and 2. Rxd8#.

15) The rook on a8 is protected by the knight. The c8 square is guarded by two pieces. Yet the queen sacrifice 1. Qxa8+ solves the puzzle by removing both defenders! 1. ... Nxa8 and 2. Rc8#.

16) Another queen sacrifice: 1. Qh8+ Nxh8 and 2. Rxh8#.

17) Here White has "tripled" on the e-file. 1. Re8+ Rxe8 2. Rxe8+ Rxe8 and 3. Qxe8#.

18) 1. Rh4+ Rxh4 2. Rxh4+ Rxh4 and 3. Qxh4#.

19) White needs to give up the queen again: 1. Qc8+ Rxc8 2. Rxc8+ Rxc8 and 3. Rxc8#, as the bishop on e3 guards the escape on a7.

20) Another queen sacrifice: 1. Qh8+ Kxh8 2. Rf8+ Rxf8 3. Rxf8#.

12

INTERMEDIATE MOVES

Although intermediate moves are very important, the subject is often overlooked in chess training. In this chapter you will find some intermediate move exercises. The first ones are easier, while those at the end are more difficult.

An intermediate move is an "in-between" move that helps set up a very good follow-up move. In order to help you with the exercises in this chapter, I will give you hints to get your mind to focus in the right direction.

This is the one type of tactical motif that I am glad I learned at a very early age. It really helped me stay ahead of the competition. I taught my sisters the same thing when they started to play, and I have followed the same method in my teaching over the years.

1. White to move. If White plays 1. Nxf5 Black replies 1. ... Bxb4 and the game would be even. With an intermediate move, White can win a piece. What is this move?

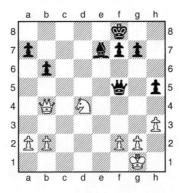

2. White to move. Both queens are under attack. What should White do to win a piece?

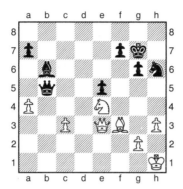

3. White to move. Both rooks are under attack. What should White do to win a piece?

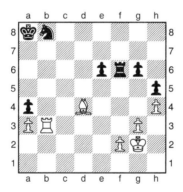

4. White to move. Find the move for White that wins a piece.

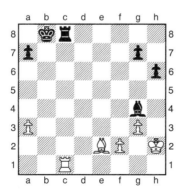

5. White to move. Both bishop and knight are under attack. But the correct intermediate move nets White a piece. What is this move?

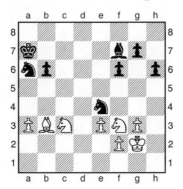

6. White to move. Both queens are under attack. What should White do to win a piece?

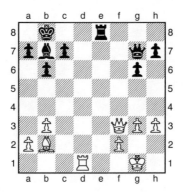

7. White to move. Both queens are under attack. White should White do to win the queen?

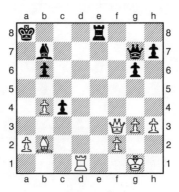

8. White to move. The White queen is attacking the Black rook. But the problem is that Black is threatening mate. What should White do to win the rook?

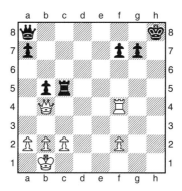

9. White to move. White wants to capture the rook on d8. How can White do that without getting mated on the back rank?

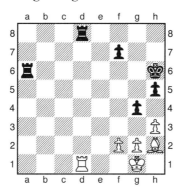

10. White to move. White wants to capture the bishop on c4 but has to be careful about the fork on g4 by the Black knight. What should White do to win?

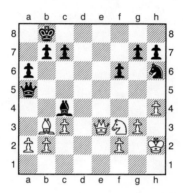

11. White to move. What should White play to win a piece?

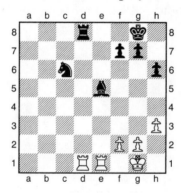

12. White to move. White wants to capture the Black rook on d8. The problem is that Black is threatening mate on g2. How does White avoid this and win the rook?

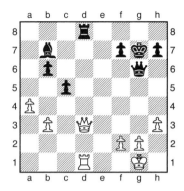

13. Black to move. Both bishops are under attack. What should Black play to win?

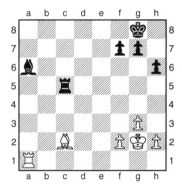

14. Black to move. White is one move away from promoting the h-pawn. How can Black stop it?

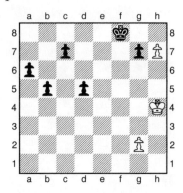

15. Black to move. Both queens are under attack. How can Black win?

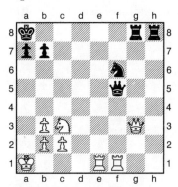

16. Black to move. The right intermediate move wins a rook.

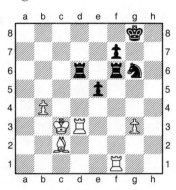

17. White to move. What can White do to win a piece?

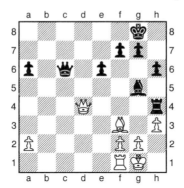

18. White to move. The Black knight is under attack. But Black is threatening a discovery with … Bxa2+, winning the queen. How should White handle this and win?

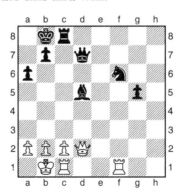

19. White to move. White is facing a checkmate threat of … Qa1#. Can White solve this problem and win the Black rook on d6 at the same time?

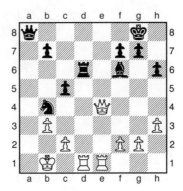

20. White to move. White's queen is attacked, but with the right intermediate move, White can win a piece.

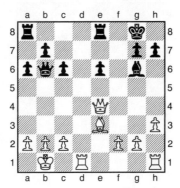

Solutions

1) 1. Qxe7+ wins a piece.

2) 1. Qxh6+ wins. But not 1. Qxb6? Qxb6.

3) 1. Rxb8+ and White wins a piece.

4) 1. Rb1+. The natural-looking 1. Rxc8+ does not work, as Black holds with 1. ... Bxc8.

5) 1. Nb5+ followed by taking the bishop on f7.

6) Sacrifice the queen: 1. Qxb7+.

7) The previous solution does not work here: 1. Qxb7+ loses to 1. ... Qxb7. However 1. Qa3+ does it.

8) After taking the rook with 1. Qxc5, Black gives mate with 1. ... Qh1#. That is why 1. Rh4+, followed by 2. Qxc5, makes a difference.

9) Give the White king some air with 1. Bf4+.

10) Move the queen away from the fork threat with a checking move: 1. Qe8+ and then capture the bishop.

11) The knight on c6 is overloaded (defending two pieces at the same time), so 1. Rxd8+ Nxd8 and 2. Rxe5 wins the bishop.

12) Trade queens with 1. Qxg6+ fxg6 and then 2. Rxd8.

13) 1. ... Bb7+ wins.

14) By giving up the g-pawn. 1. ... g5+ 2. Kxg5 and 2. ... Kg7.

15) 1. ... Qa5+. On the other hand 1. ... Qxf1 is not effective, as 2. Qxg8+ equalizes.

16) 1. ... Rc6+. But not 1. ... Rxd3+ 2. Bxd3 protecting the rook on f1.

17) 1. Qxh4 and if 1. ... Qxf3 2. Qxg5.

18) First play 1. Qh2+ Ka8 followed by capturing the knight by 2. Rxf6. Or if 1. ... Qc7 2.Qxc7+.

19) Yes, first by forcing the trade of queens with 1. Qe8+ Qxe8 2. Rxe8+ and then by taking the rook on d6 next.

20) 1. Qxg6 and after 1. ... Qxe3 2. Qxe8+.

13

CASTLING, UNDERPROMOTION, EN PASSANT

This category of exercises includes castling, pawn promotion to pieces other than a queen, and en passant captures. These are other parts of the game that I learned in my early training and benefited from. These moves are not stressed enough in most books, unfortunately. In solving these exercises, it will help you to remember what you learned in the tutorials earlier in this book, especially pawn promotion and the rules for castling.

The exercises in this chapter will help you recognize these special moves in your games, and this will help you win more games. Some of the moves can be tricky and hard to see, so I have added hints. The point is, in chess you have to be able to see everything and expect anything!

1. White to move and checkmate in one move. Can you find this special move? Hint: The White king on e1 and the rook on a1 have not yet moved.

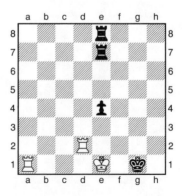

2. White to move and checkmate in one move. Hint: The White king and rook have not yet moved.

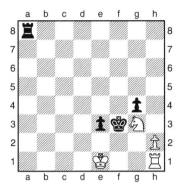

3. White to move and checkmate in one move. Hint: The White king and rook have not yet moved.

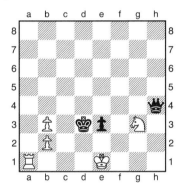

4. White to move and win a rook. Hint: The king and rook have not moved.

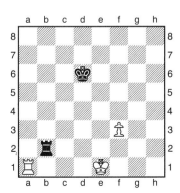

5. White to move and checkmate in one move. Can you find this special move?

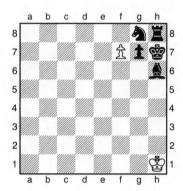

6. White to move and checkmate in one move. Where is this special move?

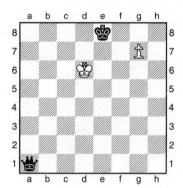

7. White to move and checkmate in one move. Can you find the right move?

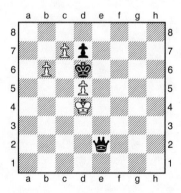

8. White to move and checkmate in one move. What is the special move?

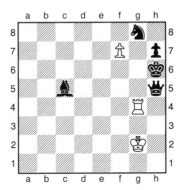

9. Black's last move was g7–g5 to block the check by the White bishop on d2. Can you find a checkmate in one move for White?

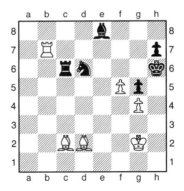

10. Black's last move was b7–b5. Can you find a checkmate for White?

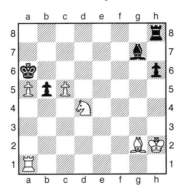

11. Black's last move was f7–f5. Can you find a checkmate in one for White?

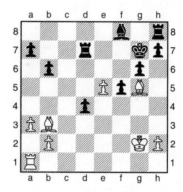

12. Black's last move was e7–e5. What should White play to win the queen?

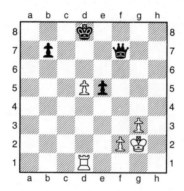

13. White's last move was e2–e4. What should Black do to win the White queen?

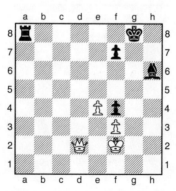

14. Black to move and win the knight. Hint: The Black king and rook have not yet moved.

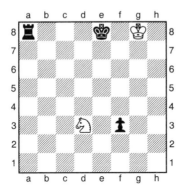

15. Black to move. Can you find the special move that forks White's king and queen?

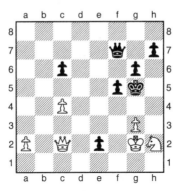

16. Black to move. What is the special move that wins the queen?

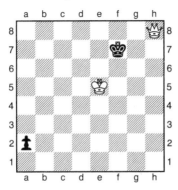

17. White to move and mate in two moves. But watch out! Promoting the pawn to a queen results in stalemate.

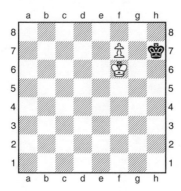

18. White to move and mate in two moves. Can you find the mate?

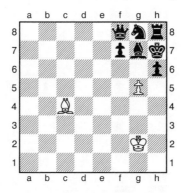

19. White to move and win the knight in two moves. Hint: The White king and rook on a1 have not moved.

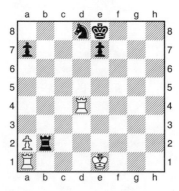

20. White to move. White is ahead in material, but Black threatens checkmate. Is there a defense for White?

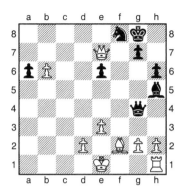

Solutions

1) Castle on the queenside with
   1. 0-0-0#!.
2) Castle on the kingside with
   1. 0-0#!.
3) Castle on the queenside with
   1. 0-0-0#!.
4) 1. 0-0-0+ checks the king and
   attacks the rook at the same
   time.
5) This is an exceptional situation.
   White can promote the pawn to
   a queen, but that is not mate.
   The best move is
   underpromotion by 1. f8=N#!.
6) Promote the pawn by
   1. g8=Q#.
7) Again you need to
   underpromote the pawn to a
   knight: 1. c8=N#!.
8) Promoting the pawn by
   1. f8=Q+ is not good because
   the Black bishop can capture it.
   The right promotion is:
   1. fxg8=N#.
9) It is very important to know
   that Black has just played
   g7-g5 because now en passant
   is allowed: 1. fxg6 e.p.#.
10) Capture en passant with
    1. axb6 e.p.#. White can
    also capture en passant with
    1. cxb6 e.p., but then Black
    would capture the White
    knight on d4.
11) While 1. Bf6+ is not a
    bad move, much better is
    1. exf6 e.p.#.

12) Play the discovered check
    1. dxe6 e.p.+.
13) Fork the king and queen with
    1. ... fxe3 e.p.+.
14) Castle on the queenside with
    1. ... 0-0-0+.
15) Promoting the pawn with
    1. ... e1=Q offers the new
    queen only a short life after
    2. Nf3+. But 1. ... e1=N+ wins
    the White queen.
16) Promoting the pawn to a queen
    by 1. ... a1=Q+ skewers the
    White king and wins the
    queen.
17) The fastest win is 1. f8=R,
    putting Black in zugzwang
    (a situation in which he has no
    good moves): after 1. ... Kh6,
    2. Rh8# ends the game. It is
    worth noting that 1. Ke7 wins
    the game too, but it takes
    longer.
18) Bd3+ forces Black to block
    the check with ... f5.
    Now en passant is possible:
    2. gxf6 e.p.#.
19) White sacrifices the exchange
    with 1. Rxd8+ Kxd8 and then
    2. 0-0-0+ checks the king and
    wins the rook.
20) Castle! 1. 0-0.

STALEMATE

Stalemate is a very important defensive tactical motif. It's a part of chess that is not touched on often enough in chess instruction books, which is unfortunate, because it may be able to help you save games that are otherwise lost. And it is just as important to recognize when a stalemate may spoil a winning position by turning it into a draw.

Building a strong chess foundation with so many different tactical motifs helped me become a complete player. Don't overlook defensive techniques such as stalemate. They can be very useful to you in real game situations.

1. White to move. Black is far ahead in material and has several checkmate threats. Can White save the game?

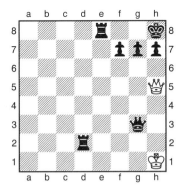

2. White to move. Black is threatening checkmate with Ra2. Can White save the game?

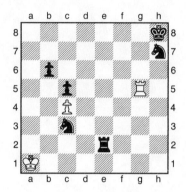

3. White to move. Black is up a rook and two pawns. Can White save the game by forcing a stalemate?

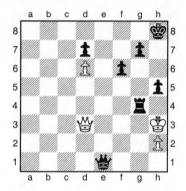

4. White to move. Black is up a queen. Is it possible for White to force a stalemate?

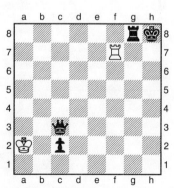

5. White to move. Black is about to give checkmate. Can White force a stalemate?

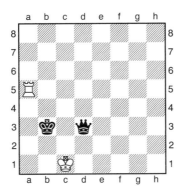

6. White to move. Black has an overwhelming material advantage. How can White save the game?

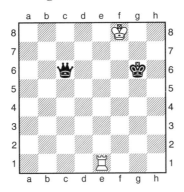

7. White to move. Black is ahead in material. Can White force a stalemate?

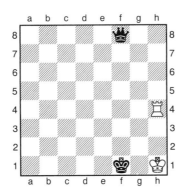

8. White to move. It looks like Black is winning. How can White save the game?

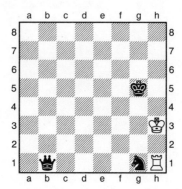

9. White to move. It seems that it's time to give up, right? Or can White force a stalemate?

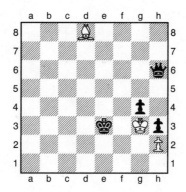

10. White to move. Black is up a Queen. How can White still save the game?

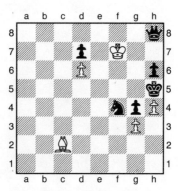

11. White to move. Black seems to have a winning position. Is it possible for White to force a stalemate?

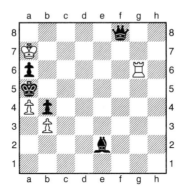

12. White to move. Black has what is usually a winning material advantage. Is it possible for White to make a draw?

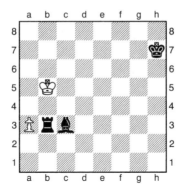

13. White threatens to play 1. g7+ and then promote the pawn. How can Black avoid losing?

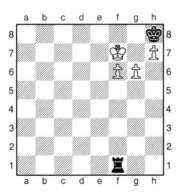

14. Black to move. Is it possible for Black to force a draw?

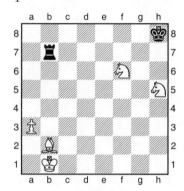

15. Black to move. White is clearly winning. Can Black force a stale-mate?

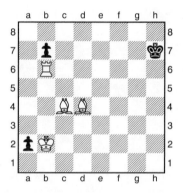

16. Black to move. Can Black force a stalemate to save the game?

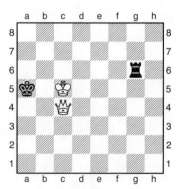

17. White to move. Can White save the game by forcing a stalemate?

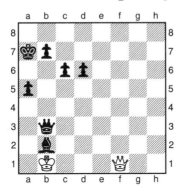

18. White to move. Black is about to promote the a-pawn to a queen. Can White create a stalemate?

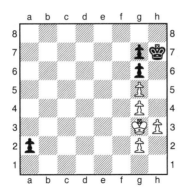

19. White to move. White is about to lose the f-pawn and eventually the game. Can White save the game by stalemate?

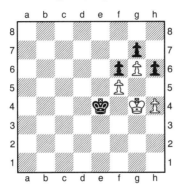

20. White to move. The White rook is pinned. Can White save the game by using stalemate?

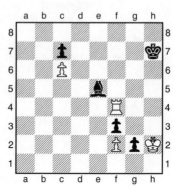

Solutions

1) The White king has no moves, but White still has a queen. Get rid of the queen with 1. Qxh7+, forcing 1. ... Kxh7, and White has no moves. Stalemate.

2) Yes, by giving up the only piece that has a legal move: 1. Rg8+ Kxg8 stalemate.

3) 1.Qh7+ forces 1. ... Kxh7 stalemate.

4) Yes, with 1. Rh7+.

5) Yes, with 1. Ra3+. If Black captures the rook, White is stalemated. On any other king move the rook captures the queen.

6) By forking Black's king and queen with 1. Re6+. Black has to take the rook (otherwise Black loses) with 1. ... Qxe6 stalemate.

7) Yes, 1. Rf4+.

8) By playing 1. Rxg1+ Qxg1 stalemate.

9) Yes, he can by forking with 1. Bg5+.

10) 1. Bg6+ is almost checkmate. Black must capture with 1. ... Nxg6 stalemate.

11) 1. Rxa6+ gives up the last piece, forcing Black to capture with 1. ... Bxa6 stalemate.

12) This is a beautiful endgame. After 1. Ka4 White either wins the rook, in which case the game is a draw because Black does not have enough material to win, or if Black moves the rook away along the b-file (1. ... Rb8), then the game ends in stalemate.

13) By playing 1. ... Rxf6+ 2. Kxf6 stalemate.

14) Yes, with 1. ... Rxb2+. If White captures the rook the game ends in stalemate. If White plays 2. Kc1, Black continues to offer the rook sacrifice along the second rank with 2. ... Rc2+ 3. Kd1 Rd2+ 4. Ke1 Re2+ 5. Kf1 Rf2+, etc., until eventually a three-fold repetition of position occurs.

15) Yes, by promoting the pawn with 1. ... a1=Q+. If White doesn't capture the queen, then Black will capture the bishop on d4 and have a better position.

16) Yes, by playing 1. ... Rc6+. Now 2. Kxc6 results in stalemate. Or after 2. Kd5 White loses the queen and the game ends in a draw also.

17) White needs to get rid of the queen. After 1. Qa6+ Black can try to escape with 1. ... Kb8 2. Qa8+ (but not 2. Qxb7+? because after 2. ... Qxb7 there is no stalemate) 2. ... Kc7 and 3. Qd8+, finally giving Black no choice but 3. ... Kxd8 stalemate.

18) This is a unique endgame. White builds a wall around his own king. 1. Kh4 allows 1. ... a1=Q, but after 2. g3 Black can do nothing to avoid stalemate.

19) Yes, White can afford to lose the f-pawn and make a draw. 1. Kh5 Kxf5 stalemate.

20) 1. Kg1 gets out of the pin. If Black captures the rook, 1. ... Bxf4, White is stalemated.

15

PERPETUAL CHECK

Perpetual check is another critical defensive part of chess. This technique is often used when a player faces a losing position. Even world-class players use this defense. It was certainly an important part of my training when I started.

In the beginning of this chapter the perpetual checks are fairly easy to recognize. Toward the end, however, you will have to find ways to create perpetual check opportunities.

1. White to move. Can you find the perpetual check for White to save the game?

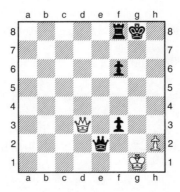

2. White to move. Black is on the verge of winning. Can White save the game?

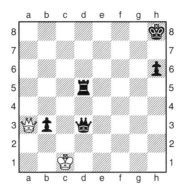

3. White to move. Black seems to have a dominating position. How can White force a draw?

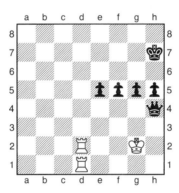

4. White to move. Black is ahead in material. Can White save the game?

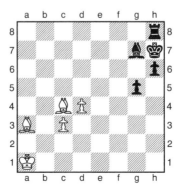

5. White to move. Black is up three pawns. How can White force a draw?

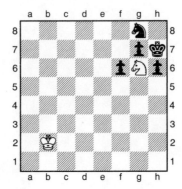

6. White to move. Black is on the verge of victory. Can White force a draw?

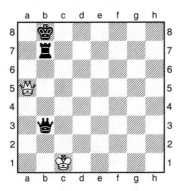

7. White to move. Black seems to have an overwhelming position. How can White force a draw by perpetual checks?

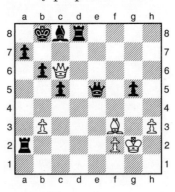

8. White to move. Black has a winning position, but White can force a draw. Can you find the perpetual checks?

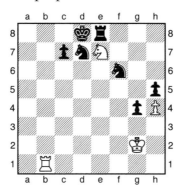

9. White to move. Black has material advantage. How can White force a draw?

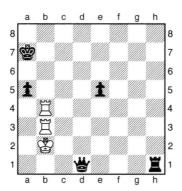

10. White to move. White is on the verge of defeat. Can White save the game?

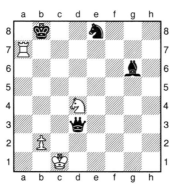

11. White to move. Black is about to checkmate White. Can you save the game for White?

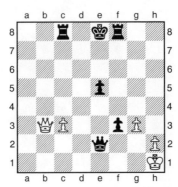

12. White to move. Look for a way for White to save the game by perpetual check.

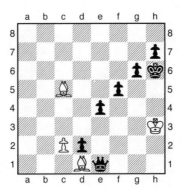

13. Black to move. Can you find a way for Black to force a draw?

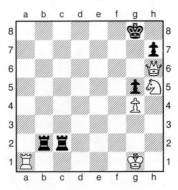

14. Black to move. Find the perpetual check that saves the game for Black.

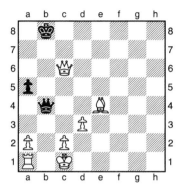

15. Black to move. Can you find the forced perpetual checks for Black?

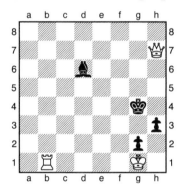

16. Black to move. Look for a way for Black to save the game by perpetual check.

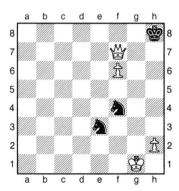

17. White to move. It seems that White cannot prevent the checkmate threats. Can you find a way for White to force a draw by perpetual check?

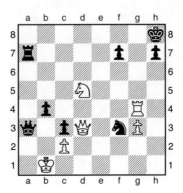

18. White to move. Can you find a way for White to force a draw?

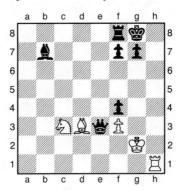

19. White to move. White is behind in material and the position seems hopeless. Can you find a way for White to force a draw by perpetual check?

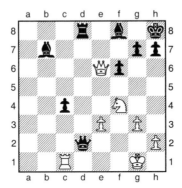

20. White to move. White is behind in material and the position seems lost. Can you find a way for White to force a draw?

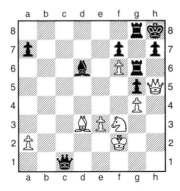

Solutions

1) 1. Qg6+. Black can only play 1. ... Kh8, 2. Qh6+ Kg8 and again 3. Qg6+, and Black cannot escape the checks.

2) Yes, with 1. Qf8+ Kh7 2. Qf7+ Kh8 3. Qf8+ and so on.

3) White needs to keep giving checks with either rook on the d6, d7, and d8 squares, starting with 1. Rd7+. Black cannot escape the perpetual checks. In fact, Black needs to be careful not to answer with 1. ... Kh6 or 1. ... Kg6 because then 2. R1d6# would follow.

4) White can force a draw with 1. Bd3+ Kg8 2. Bc4+ Kh7 3. Bd3+, etc.

5) With 1. Nf8+ Kh8 2. Ng6+ Kh7 3. Nf8+.

6) 1. Qd8+ Ka7 2. Qa5+ Kb8 3. Qd8+ and Black cannot run away from the checks.

7) By 1. Qa8+ Kc7 2. Qc6+ Kb8 3. Qa8+, etc.

8) 1. Nc6+ Kc8 2. Na7+ Kd8 3. Nc6+ forces a draw.

9) With rook checks on the b-file. 1. Rb7+ Ka8 (after 1. ... Ka6? Black gets mated with 2. R3b6#) 2. Rb8+, etc.

10) Yes, 1. Nc6+ Kc8 2. Ne7+ Kd8 3. Nc6+, and Black cannot get out of the perpetual checks.

11) 1. Qe6+ Kd8 2. Qd6+ Ke8 3. Qe6+, etc.

12) This is a really nice one! 1. Bf8+ Kg5 2. Be7+ Kf4

3. Bd6+ Ke3 4. Bc5+ Kf4 5. Bd6+, and so on.

13) The Black rooks keep giving check along the second rank, starting with 1. ... Rg2+ 2. Kf1, and now either rook can check on f2, and so on.

14) 1. ... Qe1+ 2. Kb2 Qb4+ 3. Kc1 Qe1+ draw.

15) 1. ... Bc5+ 2. Kh2 Bd6+ 3. Kg1 Bc5+, etc.

16) 1. ... Nh3+ 2. Kh1 Nf2+ 3. Kg1 Nh3+ with perpetual checks.

17) White needs to give up his queen to save the game. 1. Qxh7+ Kxh7 2. Nf6+ Kh6 (2. ... Kh8 is even worse, because of 3. Rg8#) 3. Ng8+ Kh5 4. Nf6+ draw.

18) The first move is the necessary 1. Bh7, forcing 1. ... Kh8, and then any discovered check along the b1-h7 diagonal with the bishop, such as 2. Bc2+ Kg8 3. Bh7+, and so on.

19) By sacrificing the knight: 1. Ng6+ forcing 1. ... hxg6, followed by 2. Qh3+ Kg8 3. Qe6+ Kh7 4. Qh3+ draw.

20) Another pretty queen sacrifice: 1. Qxh7+ Kxh7 2. Nxg5+ (this move is possible because the rook on g6 is pinned) 2. ... Kh6 3. Nxf7+ Kh7 4. Ng5+ and the knight moves back and forth between g5 and f7.

16

PROPER DEFENSIVE CHOICES

Chess players face tough decisions in every game. A wrong decision could cost you the game. So it is very important not only to find the correct ways to attack but also to find proper ways to defend.

It's just as important to keep your material by defending it properly as it is to gain material by attacking correctly. In this chapter you will learn how to make the correct choice of defensive moves. The right choice can save your game or can even win.

1. White to move. The Black rook is attacking the bishop and knight at the same time. What is the best defense for White?

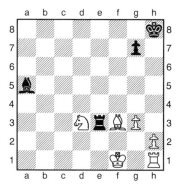

2. White to move. The Black rook is attacking the queen. What is the best defense?

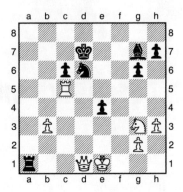

3. White to move. Black is threatening checkmate. How should White defend?

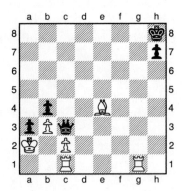

4. White to move. Black is forking the king and queen with check. What should White do?

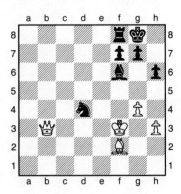

5. White to move. The Black queen is attacking both the rook and the knight. How should White defend?

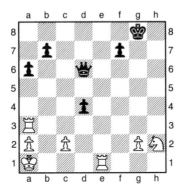

6. White to move. The Black queen is attacking both knights. How should White defend?

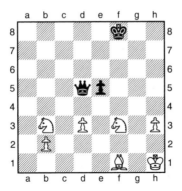

7. White to move. Black is about to checkmate White. How can White defend?

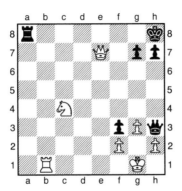

8. White to move. Black is attacking both rooks. Is there a way to defend?

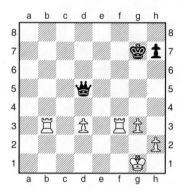

9. White to move. The White bishop is under attack and stuck in a pin. How can White defend without losing material?

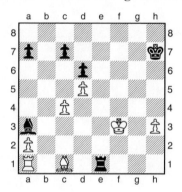

10. White to move. How can White defend the bishop and get out of check?

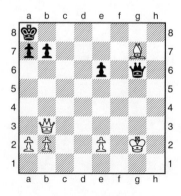

11. White to move. How can White defend against the check without losing the rook?

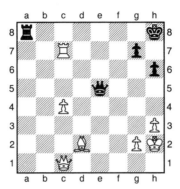

12. Black just moved the pawn from d6 to d5. Now it is White to move. Black is forking the bishop and knight. What should White do?

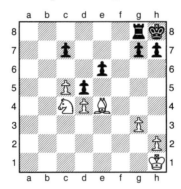

13. Black to move. The black bishop is under attack and seems to have no safe square to move to. What should Black do to save the bishop?

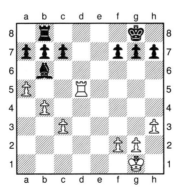

14. Black to move. How should Black defend the knight?

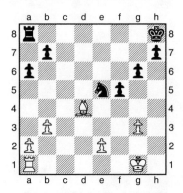

15. Black to move. What is the best defense for Black?

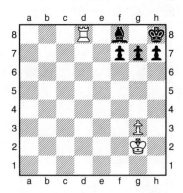

16. White to move. Where should the White king go?

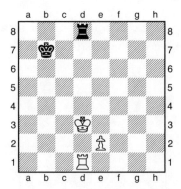

17. White to move. What is the best way for White to defend the attack
   on the rook?

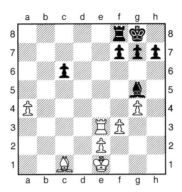

18. White to move. What is White's best move?

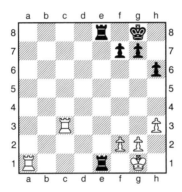

19. White to move. What should White do?

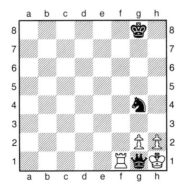

20. White to move. White is in check. How should White respond?

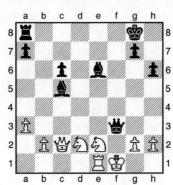

Solutions

1) The only way White can protect both pieces at once is by defending the knight with the bishop by 1. Be2. Wrong is 1. Ne1 Rxe1+.

2) White needs to guard the first rank with 1. Rc1.

3) The only move is 1. Rb1, to protect the square b2.

4) You are in check. Don't touch your king right away but instead capture the knight with 1. Bxd4.

5) Protect the knight with the rook by 1. Rh3.

6) Connect the knights with 1. Nd2.

7) White needs to guard the g2 square with 1. Ne3.

8) By playing 1. d4. It is better to lose a pawn than a rook!

9) By playing 1. Bb2, so that if 1. ... Rxa1 2. Bxa1.

10) By blocking the check with 1. Qg3.

11) 1. Bf4 does the job. The bishop blocks the check while indirectly defending the rook.

12) 1. Ne5 and the bishop cannot be taken (1. ... dxe4) because of the smothered mate with 2. Nf7.

13) Counterattack by 1. ... c6. After the rook moves away from d5, the bishop moves from b6.

14) Simply with 1. ... Re8.

15) Protect the bishop with 1. ... Kg8.

16) To 1. Kc2, to protect the rook on d1.

17) 1. Rc3 so that if 1. ... Bxc1 2 Rxc1. Other rook moves lose the bishop on c1.

18) To trade with 1. Rxe1+ Rxe1 2. Kh2.

19) Taking with the rook allows checkmate with 1. ... Nf2#. But 1. Kxg1 is good.

20) White has to take with 1. Nxf3. Taking with the pawn, 1. gxf3, is bad, as then Black checkmates with 1. ... Bh3#.

17

DEFENDING BY CHECK OR PIN

In this chapter you will learn some very important additional defensive techniques that can come in handy in game situations. They can help you save games and sometimes can even turn a loss into a win.

The exercises in this chapter are quite unusual. Even though they train you to perfect these defenses, they will often reflect a counter-offensive state of mind.

In the beginning, the examples are easy. The level of difficulty increases toward the end.

1. White to move. Black threatens 1. … Qg2#. What is the most effective move for White?

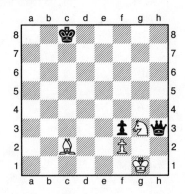

2. White to move. What is the best move for White?

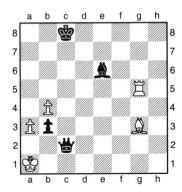

3. White to move. What should White play to defend against the check and avoid losing the rook?

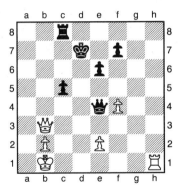

4. White to move. What should White do to protect both rooks?

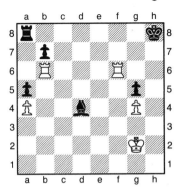

5. White to move. How should White defend against the pin of the knight?

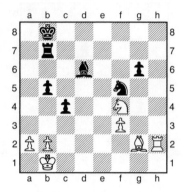

6. White to move. How can White defend against the pawn promotion?

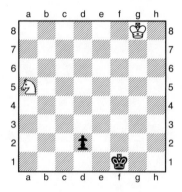

7. White to move. What can White do to stop Black from promoting the pawn?

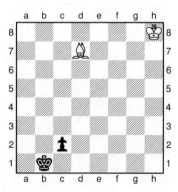

8. White to move. How can White avoid the checkmate on g2?

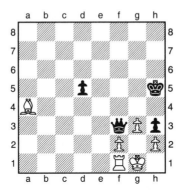

9. White to move. How can White win the Black bishop without losing the rook?

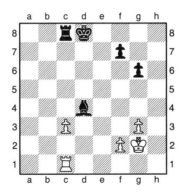

10. White to move. White is facing a fork. How can White get out of it without losing material?

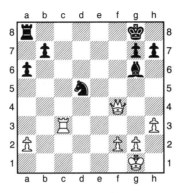

11. White to move. Black is threatening checkmate on h2. How can White avoid that?

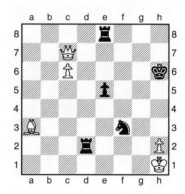

12. White to move. White is facing a devastating pin. How can White undo the pin?

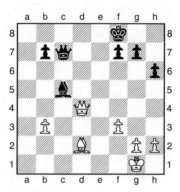

13. Black to move. White is planning to promote the pawn. How can Black stop that?

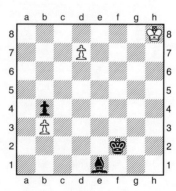

14. Black to move. White is about to promote. Can Black stop that? How?

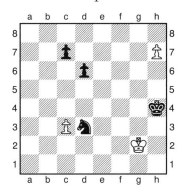

15. Black to move. How can Black stop the White pawn from promoting?

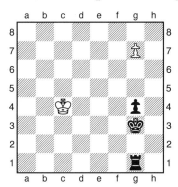

16. Black to move. How can Black defend the mate threat on g7?

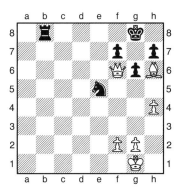

17. White to move. How can White stop the mate threat on h2?

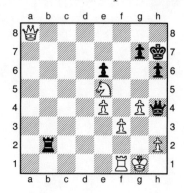

18. White to move. Can White avoid the checkmate threat on b2?

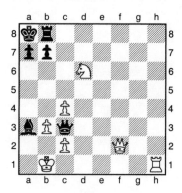

19. White to move. What should White play to stop the mate threat on g2?

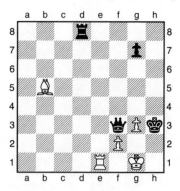

20. White to move. What is the best way to stop the mate threat and win the queen?

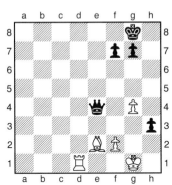

Solutions

1) Here White forks with 1. Bf5+.

2) Again White is under fire. But 1. Rc5+ saves the game.

3) Give a countercheck with 1. Qd3+.

4) Move away with check: 1. Rh6+ Kg7 and now 2. Rbg6+ and both rooks are safe.

5) Move the rook out of the pin with 1. Rh8+, which frees the knight.

6) The promotion cannot be prevented, but White can prepare to greet the new queen with 1. Nc4 and if 1. ... d1=Q then 2. Ne3+ forks king and queen.

7) By pinning it with 1. Bf5. After 1. ... Kb2, White captures the pawn with 2. Bxc2 Kxc2 and the game is a draw due to insufficient mating material.

8) 1. Bd1 pins the queen and wins it on the next move.

9) White wins the bishop by pinning it with 1. Rd1.

10) White saves the queen by pinning the knight with 1. Qc4 and then moves the rook.

11) By playing 1. Bc1 and the Black rook is pinned.

12) By the counter-pin 1. Bb4.

13) The bishop needs to get on the d8-h4 diagonal, so 1. ... Bc3+ 2. Kg8 and 2. ... Bf6 stops the pawn just in time.

14) Yes, with 1. ... Nf4+ followed by 2. ... Ng6.

15) By getting the rook to the eighth rank: 1. ... Rc1+ followed by 2. ... Rc8.

16) 1. ... Rb1+ forces 2. Kh2, and then 2. ... Ng4+ forks king and queen.

17) By a temporary queen sacrifice: 1. Qh8+ Kxh8 2. Ng6+ wins the queen back.

18) Yes, with another queen sacrifice: 1. Qxa7+ Kxa7 followed by 2. Nb5+ winning the queen back. Note that it's necessary to play Nb5 with *check*.

19) 1. Bf1+ Kg4 and then 2. Be2 pins the queen.

20) 1. Rd8+ Kh7 2. Bd3 pins the queen.

PATTERN RECOGNITION

This chapter, devoted to pattern recognition, is part of the exclusive teaching method that I have developed during my thirty-year career as competitor and teacher. The ability to recognize familiar patterns is one of the key skills that players must learn to develop in order to improve.

In this chapter I have taken certain typical checkmate patterns and developed additional positions around them. By recognizing the checkmate patterns, you will be able to solve checkmates up to six moves deep! The puzzles are easier in the beginning but become more difficult toward the end of the chapter.

1. We begin with a simple checkmate idea, and in the next two problems we see how to recognize the pattern in more fully developed forms. First, White checkmates in one move.

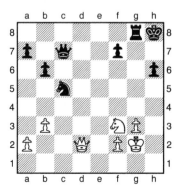

2. Using the same pattern, how can White checkmate in two moves?

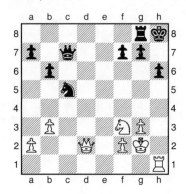

3. Using the same pattern again, how can White checkmate in three moves?

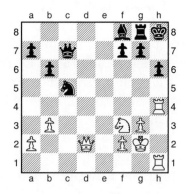

4. In this position White has a checkmate in one move. Can you find it?

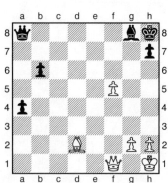

5. Using the same pattern, how can White checkmate in two moves here?

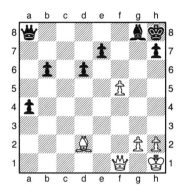

6. Using the same pattern, how can White checkmate in three moves?

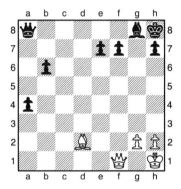

7. In this position, White has an immediate checkmate in one move. Can you find it?

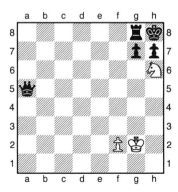

8. This is the famous smothered mate idea. How can White checkmate in two moves?

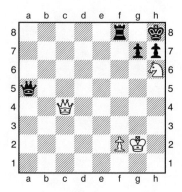

9. Using the same pattern, how can White checkmate in three moves?

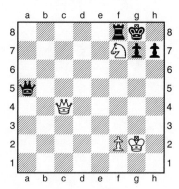

10. White to move. Can you find a checkmate in one move for White?

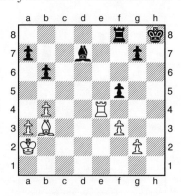

11. Using the same pattern, how can White checkmate in two moves here?

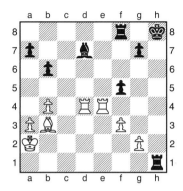

12. Using the same pattern, how can White checkmate in three moves here?

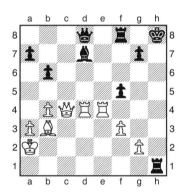

13. White has a checkmate in one move. Can you find it?

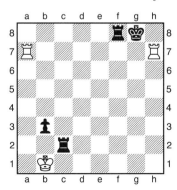

14. Using the same pattern, how can White checkmate in two moves here?

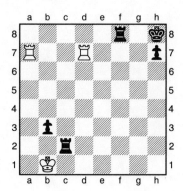

15. Using the same pattern, how can White checkmate in three moves here?

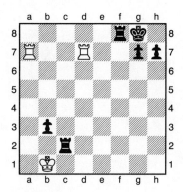

16. White to move. Can you find a checkmate in one move for White?

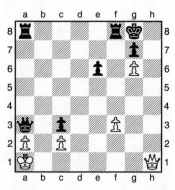

17. Using the same pattern, how can White checkmate in two moves here?

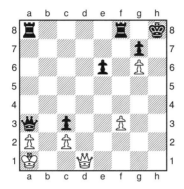

18. Using the same pattern, how can White checkmate in three moves here?

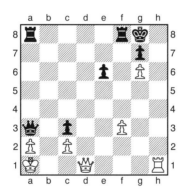

19. Using the same pattern, how can White checkmate in four moves here?

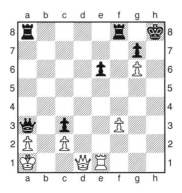

20. Using the same pattern, how can White checkmate in five moves here?

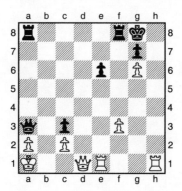

21. Using the same pattern, how can White checkmate in six moves here?

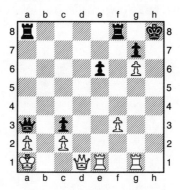

22. White has a simple checkmate in one move. Can you find it?

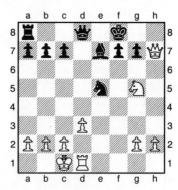

23. Using the same pattern, how can White checkmate in two moves here?

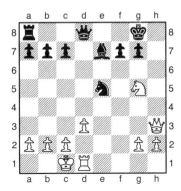

24. Using the same pattern, how can White checkmate in three moves here?

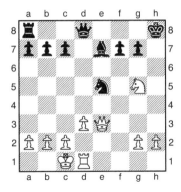

Solutions

1) 1. Qxh6#.

2) 1. Rxh6+ and 2. Qxh6#.

3) 1. Rxh6+ gxh6 2. Rxh6+ Bxh6
3. Qxh6# or 2. ... Kg7
3. Qg5#.

4) 1. Bc3#.

5) 1. Bc3+ e5 2. fxe6 e.p.#.

6) 1. Bc3+ f6 2. Qxf6+ exf6
3. Bxf6# or 1. ... e5
2. Bxe5+ f6 3. Bxf6+ or
3. Qxf6#.

7) 1. Nf7#.

8) 1. Qg8+ Rxg8 2. Nf7#.

9) 1. Nh6+ Kh8 2. Qg8+ Rxg8
3. Nf7#.

10) 1. Rh4#.

11) 1. Rh4+ Rxh4 2. Rxh4#.

12) 1. Rh4+ Rxh4 2. Rxh4+ Qxh4
3. Qxh4#.

13) 1. Rag7#.

14) 1. Rxh7+ Kg8 2. Rag7#.

15) 1. Rxg7+ Kh8 2. Rxh7+ Kg8
3. Rag7#.

16) 1. Qh7#.

17) 1. Qh1+ Kg8 2. Qh7#.

18) 1. Rh8+ Kxh8 2. Qh1+ Kg8
2. Qh7#.

19) 1. Rh1+ Kg8 2. Rh8+ Kxh8
3. Qh1+ Kg8 4. Qh7#.

20) 1. Rh8+ Kxh8 2. Rh1+ Kg8
3. Rh8+ Kxh8 4. Qh1+ Kg8
5. Qh7#.

21) 1. Rh1+ Kg8 2. Rh8+ Kxh8
3. Rh1+ Kg8 4. Rh8+ Kxh8
5. Qh1+ Kg8 6. Qh7#.

22) 1. Qh8#.

23) 1. Qh7+ Kg8 2. Qh8#.

24) 1. Qh3+ Kg8 2. Qh7+ Kf8
3. Qh8#.

SECTION II

32 KEY ENDGAME POSITIONS

There's a large misconception in American chess: that beginners should place most of their emphasis on learning the openings. While memorizing some chess openings may help you survive the beginning phase of the game, and understanding basic opening principles can also keep you out of trouble early in the game, the problem is what to do next.

I advocate that beginners concentrate on two key areas. The first is repeatedly solving tactical puzzles, and the second is studying key endgame positions. Endgames are the foundation of chess. The endgame knowledge that you acquire today will surely be useful to you half a century from now!

This chapter includes the 32 basic endgames that you will see most often in your chess-playing life. The knowledge of certain endgames is necessary to win games. Without knowledge of these winning methods, even the advantage of an extra queen could leave you frustrated and just giving checks without being able to score the point.

Unlike other chapters, where I encourage you to figure out the solutions on your own, here I recommend playing through the given positions and trying to understand the concepts. Even if you never actually encounter the rare ending of king, bishop, and knight versus king, knowing the technique of solving that ending will serve you well in the future.

In endgames, the two most important qualities are:

1. Be patient
2. Calculate accurately

The Lone King

There is one very important fact that we need to know about endgames with king and queen versus king. *The king can be checkmated only at the edge of the board.* That means either the a-file, the h-file, the first rank, or the eighth rank. If there is even a single other piece on the board for either side, the situation may change entirely.

1) King and Queen vs. King

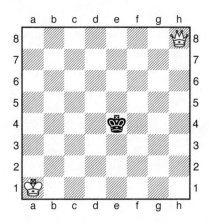

Look at the diagram. The Black king is on e4, right in the middle of the board. Knowing that the king can be mated only at the edge of the board, your priority is to force the king there. Here is the game plan:

STEP 1) Use the White queen to force the Black king to the edge of the board.

STEP 2) Cut off all escapes to make sure it stays there.

STEP 3) Bring the White king to help. *The queen cannot checkmate all by itself!*

STEP 4) Checkmate!

Step 1) 1. Qf6

White puts the Black king in a "box." Now the king cannot cross the f-file or the sixth rank.

1. … Kd5. The king stays in the middle as long as it can.

Step 2) 2. Qe7

Tightening the belt, making the box smaller.

2. … Kd4 3. Qe6 Kd3 4. Qe5 Kc4 5. Qd6 Kc3 6. Qd5 Kc2 7. Qd4 Kc1

Play over these moves carefully and see how the Black king is forced to the edge of the board. Now we have to make sure it stays there.

Step 3) 8. Qf2 Kd1

Steps 1 and 2 have been accomplished. The king is trapped on the first rank and cannot get out.

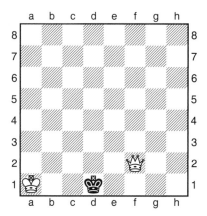

Here is the tricky part! It is time for Step 3: to bring the White king to help in the checkmate. But how? The White king needs to be brought up to the third rank, to c3 or d3. Is 9. Kb2 a possible move? Oops!!! That would be stalemate and a big no-no, spoiling a winning game and achieving only a draw! Always make sure that the opponent's king has at least one square to move to.

The right move is **9. Ka2!**

Now Black can only wait.

9. ... Kc1 10. Kb3 Kd1 11. Kc3 Kc1

Now comes **Step 4:** White can choose to checkmate with either
12. Qc2#, 12. Qe1#, 12. Qf1#, or **12. Qg1#.**

When I was a child I found this to be the easiest method to checkmate with the queen. It was how I taught my sisters, and later my students. Even today I think this is the most systematic method, and I
recommend it for all beginners or intermediate players.

Nevertheless, I must add that it is not the *shortest* method. The shortest road to checkmate after the first two moves is: 3. Kb2 Kd5 4. Kc3 Kc6
5. Kc4 Kb6 6. Qd7 Ka6 7. Kc5 Ka5 8. Qb5#. The main difference between the two is that in my preferred method, the king comes to help
only at the very end, while in the other method the king is involved
sooner. The most important advice: *Avoid stalemate! Make sure you leave
the enemy king at least one square to move to!*

2) King and Rook vs. King

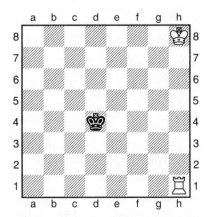

The goal is the same here as in the king and queen vs. king endgame.
The stronger side needs to force the solo king to the edge of the board.
Here, though, compared with the previous endgame, it is necessary for
the White king to help from the very beginning.

1. Kg7 Ke5 2. Rh4

Cutting off the king from the fourth rank.

2. … Kd5 3. Kf6 Kd6 4. Rh5

Further limiting the Black king's mobility.

4. … Kd7 5. Rd5+ Kc6

After 5. … Ke8 White's rook makes a quiet waiting move on the d-file, 6. Rd4, 6. Rd3, 6. Rd2 or 6. Rd1. Black is in then in zugzwang and has only one legal move, 6. … Kf8, and White checkmates with 7. Rd8#.

6. Ke6 Kc7 7. Rd6

Again similar to king and queen vs. king; White keeps limiting the mobility of the Black king.

7. … Kc8 8. Rd7

Mission accomplished! The Black king has now been pushed to the edge of the board.

8. … Kb8 9. Kd6 Kc8 10. Kc6 Kb8 11. Rd8+ Ka7

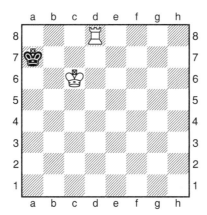

And now a waiting move along the eighth rank:

12. Re8

Black has no choice.

12. … Ka6 13. Ra8#

3) King and Two Bishops vs. King

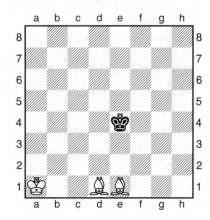

Checkmating with two bishops takes somewhat longer than with the queen or rook. The method is pretty much the same. *The two bishops work together with the king to squeeze the enemy king to the edge of the board and then to the corner.*

1. Kb2 Kd4 2. Bc3+ Ke4 3. Bc2+ Kd5 4. Kb3 Kc5 5. Bf5 Kd5 6. Kb4 Kc6 7. Kc4 Kd6 8. Bf6 Kc6 9. Be5 Kb6 10. Bd7 Ka5 11. Bc7+ Ka6

A mission accomplished—the king has been forced to the edge of the board.

12. Bc8+ Ka7 13. Kb5 Ka8

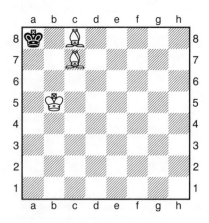

Be careful here not to stalemate with 14. Ka6 or 14. Kb6.
14. Be5 Ka7 15. Kc6 Ka8 16. Kc7 Ka7 17. Bd4+ Ka8 18. Bb7#

4) King and Two Knights vs. King

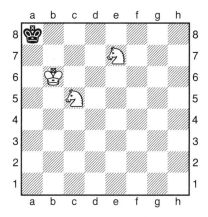

Normally, a king and two knights do not win by force against a lone king unless the two knights have some additional help, such as another extra piece or an enemy pawn to negate stalemate. The only exception is when the enemy king is already completely cornered and is about to get checkmated. In this position, the game is a draw with correct defense. All Black needs to keep in mind is to avoid the corner!

1. Ne6 Kb8 2. Nc6+ Kc8! and White cannot make progress; there is no way to force the Black king into the corner without creating stalemate. But not 2. ... Ka8?? 3. Nc7#!

5) King, Bishop, and Knight vs. King

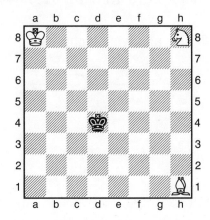

This is the most difficult of all the checkmating techniques against a lone king. The secret here is that *the weaker king has to be forced to the corner that is the same color as the bishop*. In the diagram, White has a light-colored bishop. Therefore, the Black king has to be forced to one of the light corners, either a8 or h1. If White had a dark-colored bishop, the Black king would have to be forced to a dark corner, a1 or h8.

Using all the pieces cooperatively, try to take free squares away from the king. First, squeeze the king to the edge of the board, then force it to the proper corner. The Black king, meanwhile, tries first to stay in the center and then away from the color of the bishop.

1. Ng6 Kd3 2. Kb7 Kd4 3. Kc6 Kc4 4. Bd5+ Kd4 5. Kd6 Kc3 6. Kc5 Kd3 7. Nf4+ Ke3 8. Ne6 Kd3 9. Kb4 Ke3 10. Kc3 Ke2 11. Be4 Ke3 12. Bd3 Kf3 13. Kd4 Kf2 14. Ke4 Ke1 15. Nd4 Kd2 16. Ne2

Again not letting the king escape!

16. ... Ke1 17. Ke3 Kd1

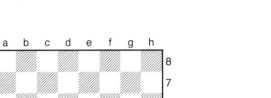

The king has been successfully forced to the back rank. The next step is to force it to the h1 corner.

18. Be4 Ke1 19. Bc2 Kf1 20. Nf4 Ke1 21. Ng2+ Kf1 22. Kf3 Kg1 23. Ne3 Kh2 24. Bf5 Kg1 25. Kg3 Kh1 26. Kf2 Kh2

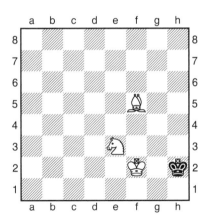

Only two more moves! Do you see how?

27. Nf1+ Kh1 28. Be4#

It seems a little confusing, doesn't it? Don't worry! I've seen very strong players unable to checkmate with the bishop and knight under time pressure. If you want to practice it, I strongly recommend you use a good chess software program such as Fritz.

King and bishop or king and knight versus the lone king with no pawns on the board is a draw.

King and Pawn Endgames

6) The "Square Rule," #1

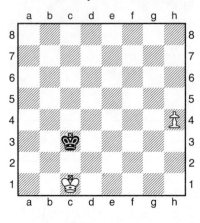

Black to move

It is crucial which player is to move in this position. If it is White's turn, White plays 1. h5 and the pawn cannot be stopped on its way to becoming a queen. But let's see what happens if it is Black's move. Besides the "square rule" (see below), you can use the counting method to see whether or not the pawn can be stopped. For example, in this position Black needs five moves to get to the promotion square, h8. The White pawn needs only four moves. With Black to move, therefore, Black can stop the pawn and save the game.

1. ... Kd4

Black has stepped into the "square" of the h-pawn. The "square of the pawn" is defined as all the squares inside the borders of d8, d7, d6, d5, d4, and e4, f4, g4, and h4. To find the square, draw an imaginary vertical line from the pawn to its promotion square and a horizontal line from the defending king to the pawn's file.

2. h5 Ke5 3. h6 Kf6 4. h7 Kg7

Just in time to stop the pawn, and the game ends in a draw.

7) The "Square Rule," #2

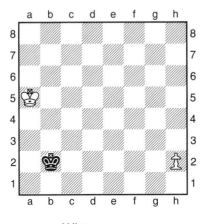

White to move

This is a tricky one. You need to remember that when a pawn is still in its initial position it can move *two* squares ahead. In the diagram, therefore, with White to move, the Black king will not be able to catch the h-pawn.

1. h4 Kc3 2. h5 Kd4 3. h6 Ke5 4. h7 Kf6 5. h8=Q+ and White wins.

8) King and Pawn on the 6th vs. King, #1

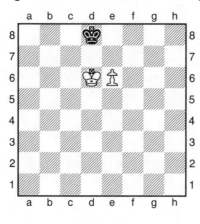

White to move

Again, it is decisive whose move it is. Here, however, it is not a pleasure to have the obligation to move. With Black to move, after 1. ... Ke8, trying to stay on the White pawn's promotion square, White pushes the pawn to e7. Black has no other move than 2. ... Kf7, when after 3. Kd7 the pawn will become a queen. However, it is White's turn in the diagram position, and Black can hold the position to a draw with correct defense:

1. e7+ Ke8 and now **2. Ke6** is stalemate.

9) King and Pawn on the 6th vs. King, #2

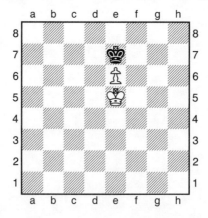

Black has three places to move his king, but only one is good enough to draw.

1. ... Ke8!

1. ... Kd8 2. Kd6 Ke8 3. e7 Kf7 4. Kd7 and White wins; or **1. ... Kf8 2. Kf6 Ke8 3. e7 Kd7 4. Kf7** and again White wins.

2. Kd6 Kd8 and we reach the previous diagram position with White to move. The position is a draw as shown above.

10) The "Opposition," #1

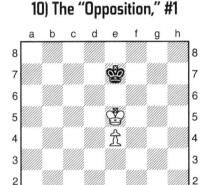

White to move draws; Black to move loses

The White king is right in front of its pawn. The two kings are opposed to each other on the same file, separated by one square. This means that whichever side *does not* have the move has the opposition. It also means that whichever player has the move must retreat and *lose* the opposition. If it is Black's turn, White wins as follows: **1. ... Kd7 2. Kf6 Ke8 3. Ke6 Kd8 4. e5 Ke8 5. Kd6 Kd8 6. e6 Ke8** and **7. e7.** If it is White's move, White must give up the opposition and can only draw:

1. Kd5 Kd7

The only right move to maintain the opposition.

2. e5 Ke7 3. e6 and now **3. ... Ke8! 4. Kd6 Kd8 5. e7+ Ke8 6. Ke6,** stalemate.

11) The "Opposition," #2

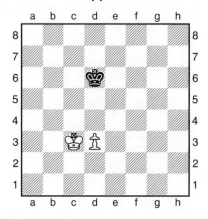

What is the only winning move for White? **1. Kd4!** gaining the opposition.

1. ... Kd7 2. Kd5 Ke7 3. Kc6 Kd8 4. d4 Kc8 5. d5 Kd8 6. Kd6! Ke8 7. Kc7 and the pawn gets through.

12) Pawn Race, #1

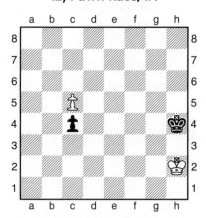

Both pawns are three moves away from the promotion square. Whoever moves first wins. **1. c6 c3 2. c7 c2 3. c8=Q** and the new White queen catches its rival.

13) Pawn Race, #2

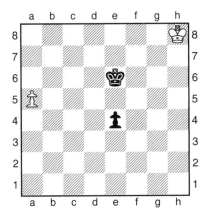

Here again, both pawns will promote at the same time, but after **1. a6 e3 2. a7 e2 3. a8=Q e1=Q,** now comes the skewer: **4. Qe8+** winning the queen.

Under normal circumstances, king and queen versus king and queen is a simple draw. The last two positions were some possible exceptions.

14) King With Extra Pawn

In king and pawn endgames with several pawns on the board, the side with an extra pawn usually wins quite easily, except possibly when the weaker side has a dangerous passed pawn.

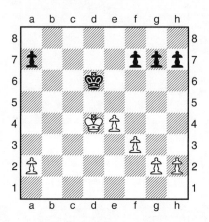

White to move and win

1. e5+ Ke6 2. Ke4 h5 3. f4 g6 4. g3 a6 5. h3 a5 6. g4 hxg4 7. hxg4 a4 8. f5+ gxf5+ 9. gxf5+ Ke7 10. Kd5 Kd7 11. a3 Ke7 12. Kc6 Ke8 13. f6 Kd8 14. Kd6 Ke8 15. Kc7 Kf8 16. Kd7 Kg8 17. Ke7 and Black loses the f-pawn.

15) Breakthrough

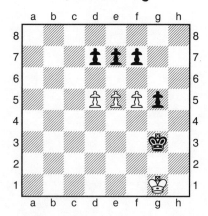

Here Black has an extra pawn, but it is White's turn to play and White wins! After **1. e6! dxe6** (or 1. ... fxe6 2. d6! exd6 3. f6) **2. f6 exf6 3. d6,** White creates an unstoppable passed pawn, reaching a winning endgame.

16) Distant Passed Pawn

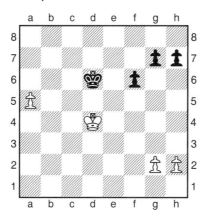

White to play and win

White wins because of the "distant" passed pawn. That pawn (on the a-file) will be used as a sacrifice to lure the Black king away from defending the kingside pawns.

1. a6 Kc6 2. a7 Kb7

Now the White king can march in and pick up the unprotected Black pawns.

3. Kd5 Kxa7

3. ... f5 4. Ke5 Kxa7 5. Kxf5 Kb6 6. Ke6 Kc5 7. Kf7 g5 8. Kg7 h5 9. Kg6 or 4. ... g6 5. Kf6 f4 6. h4 Kxa7 7. Kg7.

4. Ke6 h5 5. Kf7 and the pawns fall.

King and Major Piece versus King and Pawn

17) King and Queen vs. King and a–Pawn

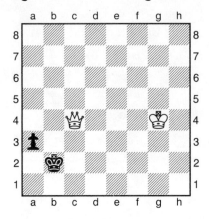

If it is White's turn to move here, White wins simply by 1. Qb4+ Ka2 2. Kf3 and Black is in zugzwang and loses the a-pawn. On the other hand, if it is Black's turn to move, Black can surprisingly save the game:

1. ... a2 2. Qb4+ Kc2 3. Qa3 Kb1 (threatening to promote the pawn) **4. Qb3+ Ka1**

Finally, White has succeeded in forcing the Black king in front of the pawn, but White has no time to bring the king to help:

5. Kf3. stalemate.

In Diagram 17, White could have won only if the king was much closer to the a-pawn; on a5, b5, c5, d5, e4, e3, e2, or e1.

18) King and Queen vs. King and c-Pawn

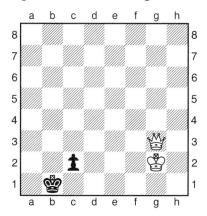

This is also a drawn position. Black keeps threatening to queen the c-pawn while White is unable to force the Black king in front of the pawn. After **1. Qb3+** Black can move to **1. ... Ka1!** because if White takes the pawn with **2. Qxc2,** it's stalemate!

19) King and Queen vs. King and b-Pawn

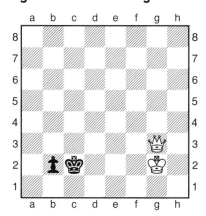

White to move and win

If the weaker side has a b-, d-, e-, or g-pawn, even if the pawn has reached the second rank and the stronger side's king is far away, the position is a win for the side with the queen.

1. Qg6+ Kc1

After 1. ... Kc3 2. Qb1, the pawn is blocked. Then all White needs to do is to bring the king close to the b-pawn for a simple win.

2. Qc6+ Kd2

If the king moves under the pawn by 2. ... Kb1, then the White king has time to come closer to the queenside with 3. Kf2.

3. Qb5 Kc2 4. Qc4+ Kd2 5. Qb3! Kc1 6. Qc3+!

Forcing the king in front of its pawn so it can't advance.

6. ... Kb1 7. Kf3

Time for White to bring in the king.

7. ... Ka2 8. Qc2 Ka1 9. Qa4+ Kb1

Again the Black king is under the pawn, so White can come closer with the king again.

10. Ke2 Kc1 11. Qd1#.

20) King and Queen vs. King and e-Pawn

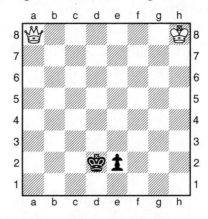

Here White wins with the same technique as in the previous example.

1. Qa5+ Kd1 2. Qa1+ Kd2 3. Qd4+ Kc2 4. Qe3 Kd1 5. Qd3+ Ke1 6. Kg7 Kf2 7. Qd2 Kf1 8. Qf4+ Kg2 9. Qe3 Kf1 10. Qf3+ Ke1 11. Kf6 Kd2 12. Qf2 Kd1 13. Qd4+ Kc2 14. Qe3 Kd1 15. Qd3+ Ke1 16. Ke5 Kf2 17. Qd2 Kf1 18. Qf4+ Kg2 19. Qe3 Kf1 20. Qf3+ Ke1 21. Kd4 Kd2 22. Qd3+ Ke1 23. Ke3 wins the pawn and, in a few moves, the game.

21) King and Rook vs. King and Pawn

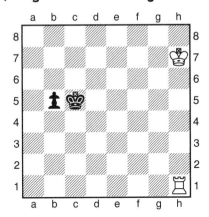

Under normal circumstances, king and rook versus king and one pawn is an easy win for the side with the rook. But when the stronger side's king is far away from the weaker side's passed pawn, the game often becomes a close race.

With accurate play in Diagram 21, Black is able to promote the b-pawn and force White to give up the rook for Black's new queen.

1. Kg6

Black plans to advance the b-pawn assisted by the king. It is urgent, therefore, for White to try to bring the White king closer to where the action is.

1. ... b4 2. Kf5

This a critical moment. Obviously, Black needs to bring the king forward. But where?

2. ... Kd4!

This is the only correct move. Black uses the concept of "shouldering." This means White advances according to plan, blocking the enemy king's route (e4, in this case) at the same time. After the more natural-looking 2. ... Kc4, Black loses: 3. Ke4 Kc3 4. Ke3 b3 5. Rc1+ Kb2 6. Kd2 Ka2 7. Rh1 (after 7. Kc3? Black has a cute escape: 7. ... b2 8. Rc2 Ka1 9. Rxb2, stalemate) 7. ... b2 8. Kc2.

3. Kf4 b3 4. Rb1 Kc3 5. Ke3 b2 6. Ke2 Kc2 draw.

22) King and Two Pawns vs. King and Rook

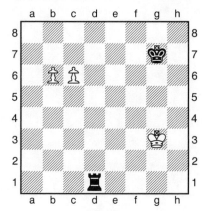

This is an important position to know. *Two connected passed pawns that have reached the sixth rank cannot be stopped by a rook alone.* Here, even though it is Black's move, Black cannot save the game. **1. ... Rb1 2. b7** (2. c7 also wins) **Kf7 3. c7** and one of the two pawns will promote.

Two Unique Endgames

23) King, Bishop, and Rook-Pawn in the "Wrong" Corner

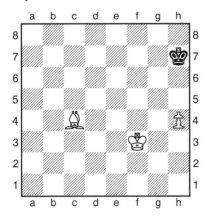

This is another must-know endgame. Although White is a bishop and a pawn ahead, the pawn's promotion square is the opposite color of the bishop. This means that White will never be able to force the Black king out of the corner. Note that this rule is valid only with the rook pawns. If White had a bishop on dark squares (for example, on c5 instead of c4) White would win easily. But here there is no win: **1. Kg4 Kg7 2. Kg5 Kh7 3. h5 Kg7 4. h6+ Kh7 5. Kh5 Kh8 6. Kg6,** stalemate.

24) King, Knight, and Rook-Pawn vs. King

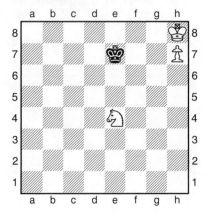

This is another surprising exception. White is a knight and a pawn ahead and the White pawn is only one square from promotion, yet Black can save the game. The trick is that after **1. ... Kf7** the White King cannot get out of the corner. **2. Nd6+ Kf8 3. Nf5 Kf7 4. Ne7 Kf8!** and White cannot make progress. However it is important to note that 1. ... Kf8 loses after 2. Nd6 and Black is in zugzwang.

In this endgame the drawing rule is: *Move the king on the same color square as the knight!*

Rook Endgames

25) King and Rook-Pawn vs. King and Rook, #1

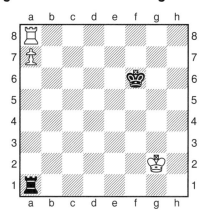

Black to move

White's problem is how to promote the a-pawn. If it were White's move, it would be easy: 1. Rf8+ Kg7 and 2. a8=Q. But it is *Black* to move.

1. ... Kg7!

The only correct square. After 1. ... Kf7 White can win with 2. Rh8! Rxa7 3. Rh7+ skewering the rook. Now if the White rook tries to move out of a8, say 2. Rb8, then the pawn remains undefended and Black can take it with 2. ... Rxa7.

2. Kf3

Now Black can just make waiting moves, either with the rook along the a-file or by moving back and forth with the king between h7 and g7.

2. ... Kh7 3. Ke4 Kg7 4. Kd5 Kh7 5. Kc6 Kg7 6. Kb6

Now that the White king is protecting the pawn, White threatens to move the rook from a8 and promote the pawn. Black must therefore start giving checks to chase the White king away.

6. ... Rb1+ 7. Ka6 Ra1+ 8. Kb7 Rb1+ 9. Kc7 Rc1+ 10. Kd6 and the rook goes back behind the pawn.

10. ... Ra1

White cannot improve his position. Draw.

26) Philidor's Position (King and Rook-Pawn vs. King and Rook, #2)

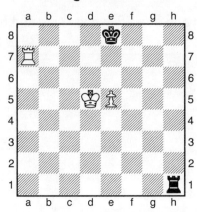

Black to play. Draw.

This is the famous Philidor position. White has an extra pawn but Black can save the game as follows:

1. ... Rh6

Keeping the rook on the sixth rank, to stop the White king's advance.

2. Rb7 Rg6

As soon as White pushes the pawn with

3. e6

Black needs to play

3. ... Rg1

to be able to give checks from behind after

4. Kd6 Rd1+ 5. Ke5 Re1+ 6. Kf6 Rf1+ draw.

27) Lucena's Position

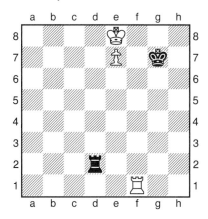

White to play and win

The Lucena position is the second most famous and fundamental rook endgame. White has a pawn that is about to be promoted; however, its own king is in the way. White's task is therefore to get the king safely out of the way so the pawn can promote. The clever solution was found by the Italian master, Lucena.

1. Rg1+ Kh7

Now after the direct 2. Kf7 Rf2+ White will only be able to hide from the rook checks back on e8. Otherwise, for example, 3. Ke6 Re2+ 4. Kd6 Rd2+ 5. Kc5 Rc2+ 6. Kd4 and now 6. ... Re2 wins the pawn.

There are two winning methods:

A) **2. Rg4**

This is the "bridge-building" method.

2. ... Rd1 3. Kf7 Rf1+ 4. Ke6 Re1+ 5. Kf6 Rf1+ 6. Ke5 Re1+ 7. Re4 and White wins.

B) **2. Ra1 Kg7 3. Ra8 Rd1 4. Rd8 Re1 5. Kd7 Rd1+ 6. Kc6 Rc1+ 7. Kb5 Rb1+ 8. Ka4 Ra1+ 9. Kb3 Rb1+ 10. Ka2** and Black runs out of checks.

Queen Endgames

28) The Wheel of Checks

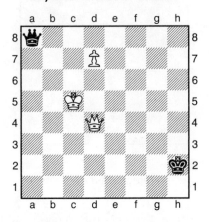

Black to move. Can White win?

In queen-and-pawn endgames, the big question always is: Can the stronger side's king hide from the eternal checks of the weaker side's queen so that the pawn can finally be promoted?

1. ... Qa7+ 2. Kc4 Qa4+ 3. Kc3 Qa1+ 4. Kd3 Qd1+ 5. Ke3 Qg1+ 6. Ke4 Qg4+ 7. Ke5 Qg7+

This is a perfect example of the "wheel of checks." White constantly has to protect the queen on d4 as well as the pawn on d7. The king cannot hide and also promote the pawn.

29) Queen Endgame With Extra Pawn

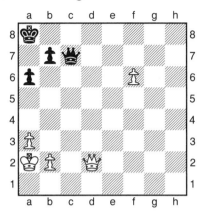

White is a pawn ahead and has a far advanced f-pawn. The White queen needs to help the pawn advance.

1. Qd5!

Keeping the king safe by stopping any checks and also threatening to advance the pawn.

1. ... Ka7 2. f7 Qe7 3. Qd4+ b6

After 3. ... Ka8 4. Qh8+ Ka7, the pawn promotes: 5. f8=Q Qe6+ 6. b3 Qe2+, and White can block further checks with 7. Qb2.

4. Qf2 Qf8 5. Qf5 a5 6. Qd7+ Ka6 7. Qe8 Qc5 8. Qa8+

Not 8. f8=Q? Qd5+ 9. b3 Qd2+ with perpetual check!

8. ... Kb5 9. f8=Q Qc4+ 10. Kb1 Qd3+ 11. Ka1 Qd1+ 12. Ka2 and Black runs out of checks.

Bishop Endgames

30) Bishops of the Same Color

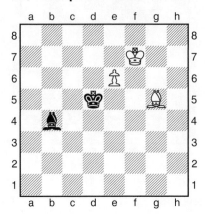

White to move and win

White's passed pawn will become a new queen when it reaches the eighth rank. First, however, it must pass the seventh rank, where Black's bishop stands ready to stop it. If White pushes the pawn immediately, Black will give up the bishop by capturing the pawn on e7. If Black can sacrifice the bishop for the pawn, even though White has an extra bishop, it will not be enough advantage to win the game. White must therefore advance the pawn only when the Black bishop cannot take it.

1. Be7

This offers a trade of bishops that Black cannot accept, since then the White pawn would advance unchallenged. So Black must withdraw.

1. ... Bd2

Now Black intends 2. ... Bg5 as soon as White's bishop leaves the d8-h4 diagonal.

2. Ba3

Also 2. Bf8 Bg5 and then 3. Bg7 serves the same purpose.

2. ... Bg5

Now the Black bishop tries to keep the pawn from advancing, from the d8-h4 diagonal.

3. Bb2 Ke4

Trying to get to f5, but one move to late.

4. Bf6

White wins. The pawn cannot be stopped.

31) Bishops of Opposite Colors

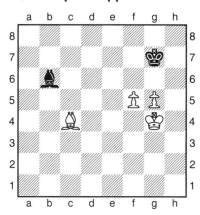

Black to move and draw

This is one of the most important illustrations of the concept that endgames with bishops of opposite colors, even if one side has several extra pawns, are often impossible to win. Keep in mind that one bishop alone cannot win.

1. ... Bd8!

The correct move. It is important to keep the White king tied to the protection of the g-pawn. White cannot improve the position. After 2. f6+ Black can just sacrifice the bishop for White's two pawns. After 2. g6 Black can play 2. ... Bf6 and then move the bishop along the a1–h8 diagonal.

Knight Endgames

32) Knight vs. Pawn

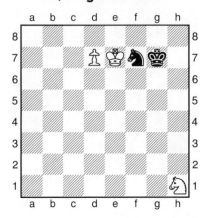

White to move and win

Knight endgames are the closest to pawn endgames. In most positions, unlike rook or queen endgames, an extra pawn is likely to guarantee a win.

How is this basic knight endgame (by Cheron 1935) to be won? At first it seems that it's high time to get the White knight out of the corner and bring it closer to the battleground. However, after a closer look we notice that after 1. Ng3 Black can force a draw with 1. ... Ne5, attacking the pawn and inviting it to promote. After 2. d8=Q Nc6+ forks the newborn queen.

The correct solution is:

1. Ke6 Nd8+ 2. Kd6 Kf6 3. Nf2 Nb7+ 4. Kc7 Ke7 5. Nd3 Nd8

If 5. ... Ke6 6. Nc5+ removing the guard.

6. Ne5 Ne6+ 7. Kc8 Kd6

If 7. ... Nd8 8. Ng6+.

8. Ng6 Kc6 9. Nf8

And the pawn will promote.

SECTION III

50 QUICK MATES IN ONE MOVE

Here are 50 one-move checkmate puzzles without hints! Solve them as quickly as you can, and then solve them again even quicker!

1. White to move

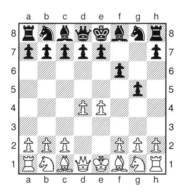

2. White to move

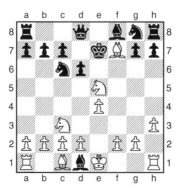

3. White to move

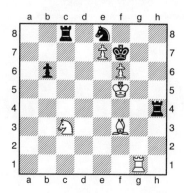

4. White to move

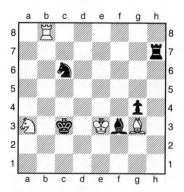

5. White to move

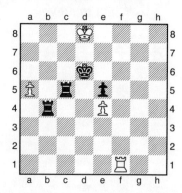

6. White to move

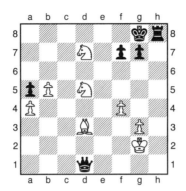

7. White to move

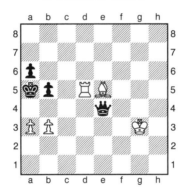

8. White to move

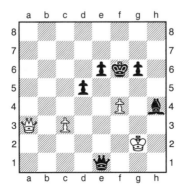

9. White to move

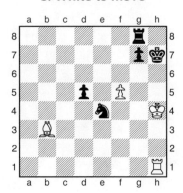

10. White to move

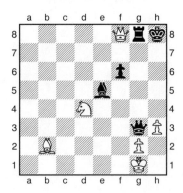

11. White to move

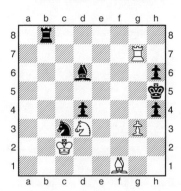

12. White to move

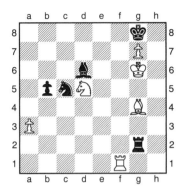

13. White to move

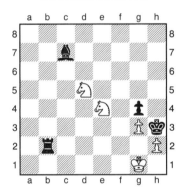

14. White to move

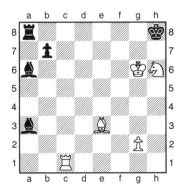

15. White to move

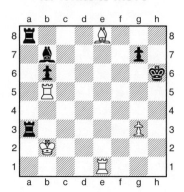

16. White to move

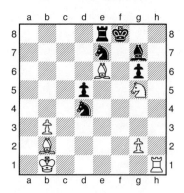

17. White to move

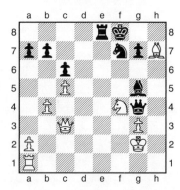

18. White to move

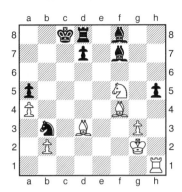

19. White to move

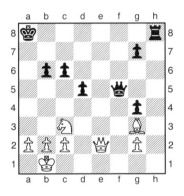

20. White to move

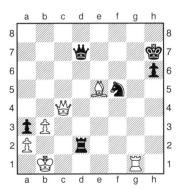

21. White to move

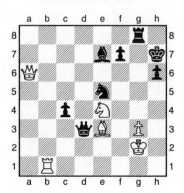

22. White to move

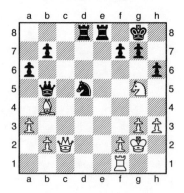

23. White to move

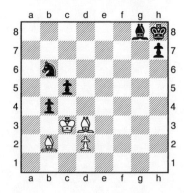

24. White to move

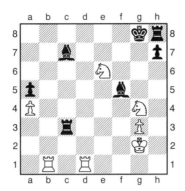

25. White to move

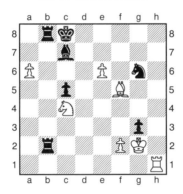

26. White to move

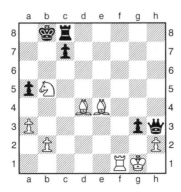

27. White to move

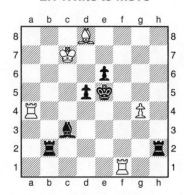

28. White to move

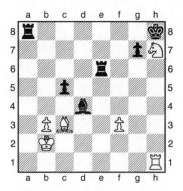

29. White to move

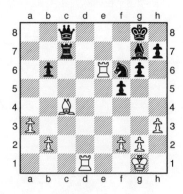

30. White to move

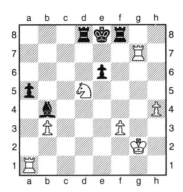

31. White to move

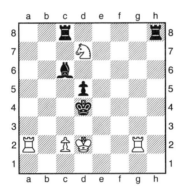

32. White to move

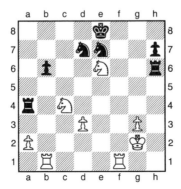

33. White to move

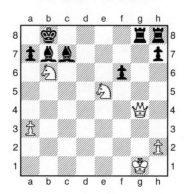

34. White to move

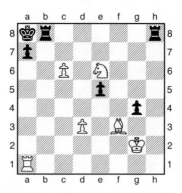

35. White to move

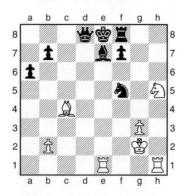

36. White to move

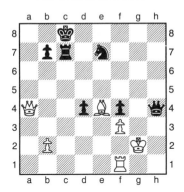

37. White to move

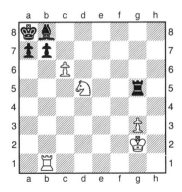

38. White to move

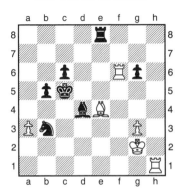

39. White to move

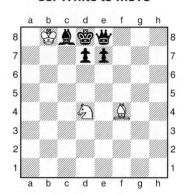

40. White to move

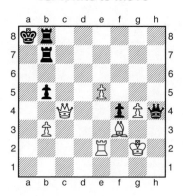

41. White to move

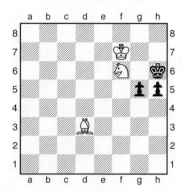

42. White to move

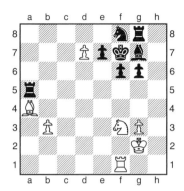

43. White to move

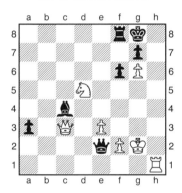

44. White to move

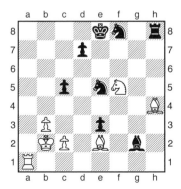

45. White to move

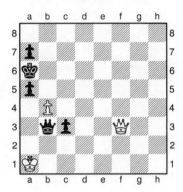

46. White to move

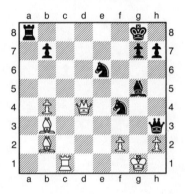

47. White to move

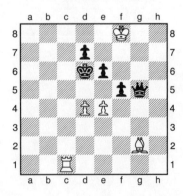

48. White to move

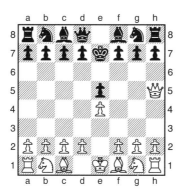

49. White to move

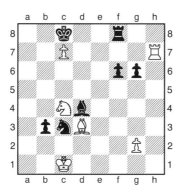

50. White to move

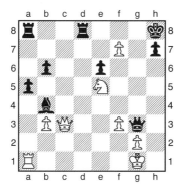

Solutions

1) 1. Qh5#.
2) 1. Nd5#.
3) 1. Bd5#.
4) 1. Be1#.
5) 1. Rf6#.
6) 1. Ne7#.
7) 1. Bc7#.
8) 1. Qf8#.
9) 1. Kg4#.
10) 1. Qh6#.
11) 1. g4#.
12) 1. Nf6#.
13) 1. Ng5#.
14) 1. Bd4#.
15) 1. Rh5#.
16) 1. Nh7#.
17) 1. Ng6#.
18) 1. Ba6#.
19) 1. Qa6#.
20) 1. Qg8#.
21) 1. Qxh6#.
22) 1. Qh7#.
23) 1. Kc2#.
24) 1. Nh6#.
25) 1. e7#.

26) 1. Ba7#.
27) 1. Bf6#.
28) 1. Nf6#.
29) 1. Re8#.
30) 1. Nc7#.
31) 1. Rg4#.
32) 1. Nd6#.
33) 1. Ned7#.
34) 1. Nc7#.
35) 1. Nf6#.
36) 1. Qe8#.
37) 1. cxb7#.
38) 1. Rxc6#.
39) 1. Bc7#.
40) 1. Ra2#.
41) 1. Ng8#.
42) 1. d8=N#.
43) 1. Ne7#.
44) 1. Nd6#.
45) 1. Qc6#.
46) 1. Qxg7#.
47) 1. e5#.
48) 1. Qxe5#.
49) 1. Nd6#.
50) 1. Ng6#.

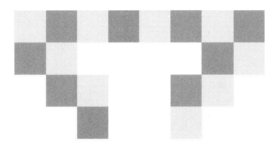

50 QUICK MATES IN TWO MOVES

This time there are 50 mates in *two moves*, again without hints! Study each position carefully and find the mate.

1. White to move

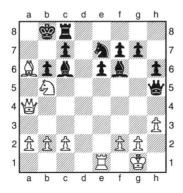

2. White to move

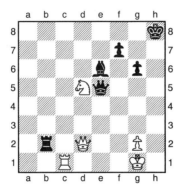

3. White to move

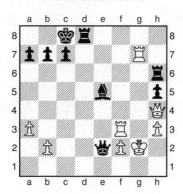

4. White to move

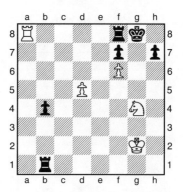

5. White to move

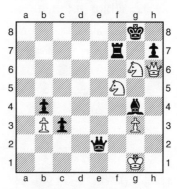

6. White to move

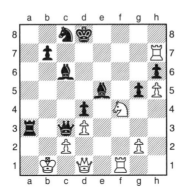

7. White to move

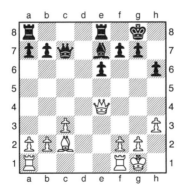

8. White to move

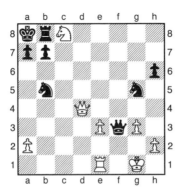

9. White to move

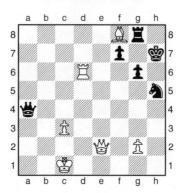

10. White to move

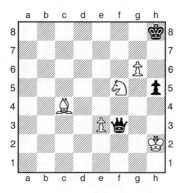

11. White to move

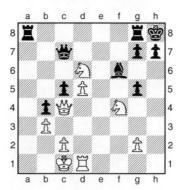

12. White to move

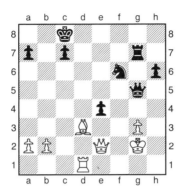

13. White to move

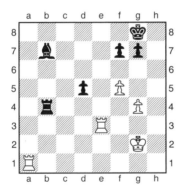

14. White to move

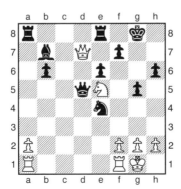

15. White to move

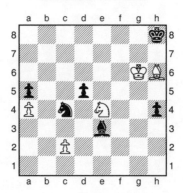

16. White to move

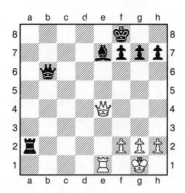

17. White to move

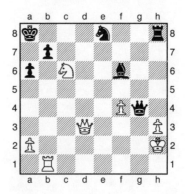

18. White to move

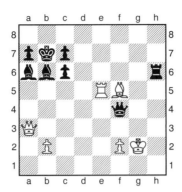

19. White to move

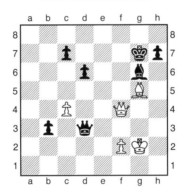

20. White to move

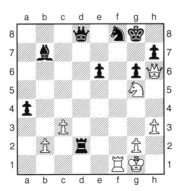

21. White to move

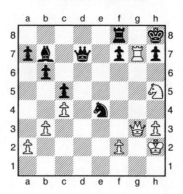

22. White to move

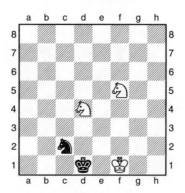

23. White to move

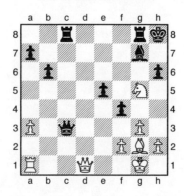

24. White to move

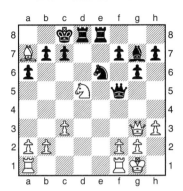

25. White to move

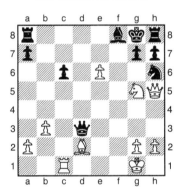

26. White to move

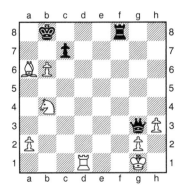

27. White to move

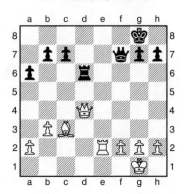

28. White to move

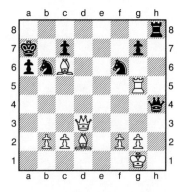

29. White to move

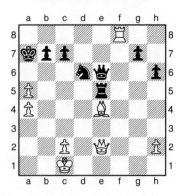

30. White to move

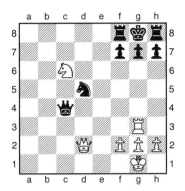

31. White to move

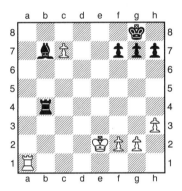

32. White to move

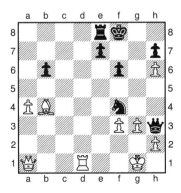

33. White to move

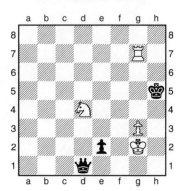

34. White to move

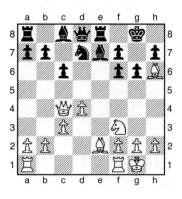

35. White to move

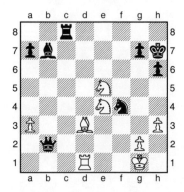

36. White to move

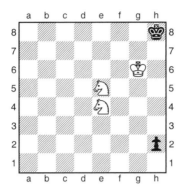

37. White to move

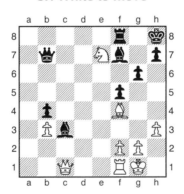

38. White to move

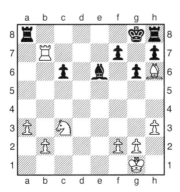

39. White to move

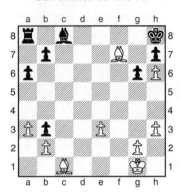

40. White to move

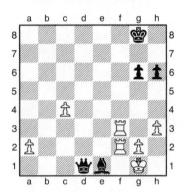

41. White to move

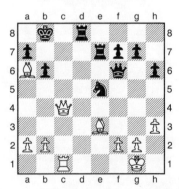

42. White to move

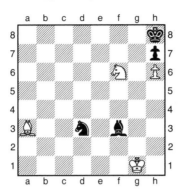

43. White to move

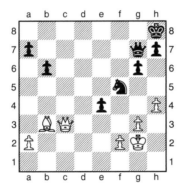

44. White to move

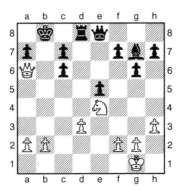

45. White to move

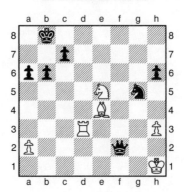

46. White to move

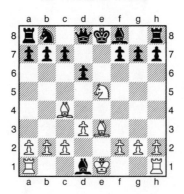

47. White to move

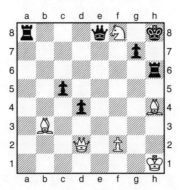

48. White to move

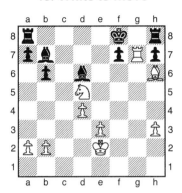

49. White to move

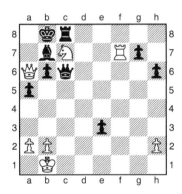

50. White to move

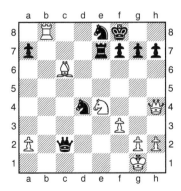

Solutions

1) 1. Bb7 followed by 2. Qa7# or 2. Qa8#.

2) 1. Qh6+ Kg8 2. Ne7#.

3) Queen sacrifice with 1. Qxd8+ Kxd8 and 2. Rf8#.

4) 1. Nh6+ Kh8 2. Rxf8#.

5) 1. Qg7+ Rxg7 2. Nh6#.

6) 1. Ne6+ Ke8 2. Rf8#.

7) 1. Qh7+ Kf8 2. Qh8#.

8) 1. Qxa7+ Nxa7 2. Nb6#.

9) 1. Qxh5+ gxh5 2. Rh6#.

10) 1. g7+ Kh7 and promotion with 2. g8=Q#.

11) 1. Ng6+ hxg6 2. Rh1#.

12) 1. Ba6+ Kb8 2. Rd8#.

13) 1. Re8+ Kh7 2. Rh1#.

14) 1. Qxf7+ Kh8 2. Ng6#.

15) 1. Bg7+ Kg8 2. Nf6#.

16) 1. Qxe7+ Kg8 2. Qe8#.

17) 1. Qxa6+ bxa6 2. Rb8#.

18) 1. Qxa6+ Kxa6 2. Bc8# or 1. ... Kb8 2. Qc8#.

19) 1. Bh6+ Kg8 2. Qf8#.

20) 1. Rxf8+ Qxf8 2. Qxh7#.

21) 1. Rxh7+ Kxh7 2. Qg7#.

22) 1. Nb3 and Black is in zugzwang. No matter where the Black knight moves, White mates with 2. Ne3#.

23) 1. Nf7+ Kh7 2. Be4#.

24) 1. Qxc7+ Nxc7 2. Nb6#.

25) 1. Qf7+ Nxf7 2. exf7#.

26) 1. Nc6+ Ka8 2. b7#.

27) 1. Re8+ Qxe8 (or 1. ... Qf8) 2. Qxg7#.

28) 1. Qxa6+ Kxa6 2. Ra5# or 1. ... Kb8 2. Qb7#.

29) 1. Qa6+ Kxa6 (or 1. ... bxa6) 2. Ra8#

30) 1. Rxg7+ Kxg7 2. Qg5#.

31) 1. Ra8+ Bxa8 2. c8=Q#.

32) 1. Qxf6+ Kg8 2. Qg7#.

33) 1. g4+ Kh6 (or 1. ... Kh4) 2. Nf5#.

34) 1. Qxf7+ Kxf7 2. Bc4# or 1. ... Kh8 2. Qg7#.

35) 1. Nf6+ Kh8 2. Nf7#.

36) 1. Nf6 h1=Q 2. Nf7#.

37) 1. Qxc3+ bxc3 2. Be5#.

38) 1. Ne4 and 2. Nf6#.

39) 1. Bd2 and 2. Bc3#.

40) 1. Rf8+ Kg7 2. R2f7#.

41) 1. Qc8+ Rxc8 2. Rxc8#.

42) 1. Bf8 and 2. Bg7#.

43) 1. Qc8+ Qg8 2. Qxg8#.

44) 1. Nc5 and 2. Qb7#.

45) 1. Rd8+ Ka7 2. Ra8#.

46) 1. Bxf7+ Ke7 2.Bg5#.

47) 1. Qxh6+ gxh6 2. Bf6#.

48) 1. Rg8+ Kxg8 2. Nf6#.

49) 1. Qa8+ Bxa8 2. Na6#.

50) 1. Qxe7+ Kxe7 or 1. ... Kg8 2. Rxe8#.

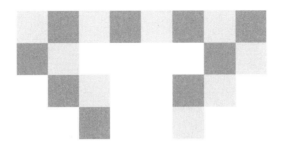

20 MATES IN THREE MOVES

These 20 *three-move* checkmate puzzles will test your ability to find more difficult checkmate patterns without hints.

1. White to move

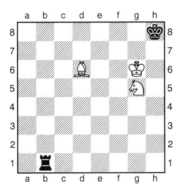

2. White to move

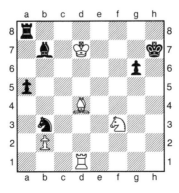

3. White to move

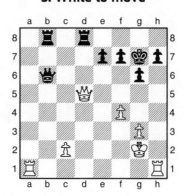

4. White to move

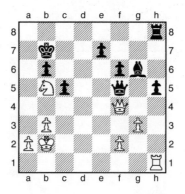

5. White to move

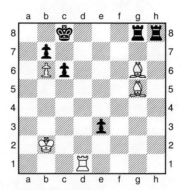

6. White to move

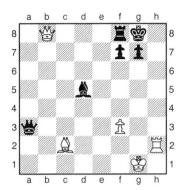

7. White to move

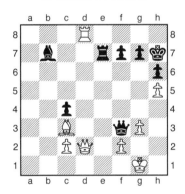

8. White to move

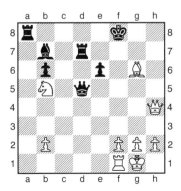

9. White to move

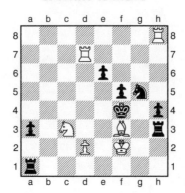

10. White to move

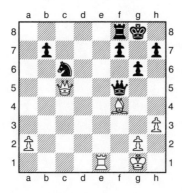

11. White to move

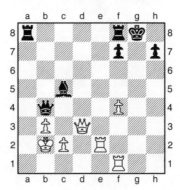

12. White to move

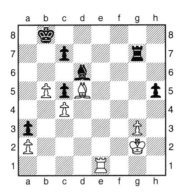

13. White to move

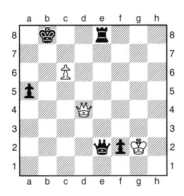

14. White to move

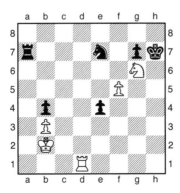

15. White to move

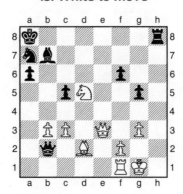

16. White to move

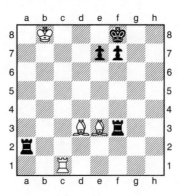

17. White to move

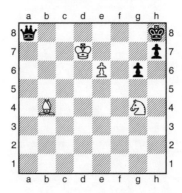

18. White to move

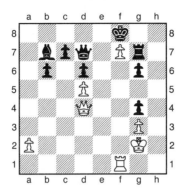

19. White to move

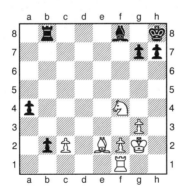

20. White to move

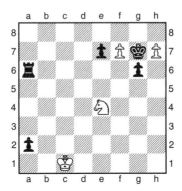

Solutions

1) 1. Nf7+ Kg8 2. Nh6+ Kh8
   3. Be5#.
2) 1. Rh1+ Kg8 2. Rh8+ Kf7
   3. Ng5#.
3) 1. Rxh7+ Kxh7 2. Qxf7+ Kh6
   3. Rh1#.
4) 1. Qc7+ Ka6 2. Qa7+ Kxb5
   3. Qa4#.
5) 1. Bf5+ Kb8 2. Bf4+ Ka8
   3. Ra1#.
6) 1. Rh8+ Kxh8 2. Qh2+ Kg8
   3. Qh7#.
7) 1. Rh8+ Kxh8 2. Qxh6+ Kg8
   3. Qxg7#.
8) 1. Qh8+ Ke7 2. Qg7+ Kd8
   3. Qf8#.
9) 1. Ne2+ Ke5 2. d4+ Kf6
   3. Rh6#.
10) 1. Qxf8+ Kxf8 2. Bh6+ Kg8
    3. Re8#.
11) 1. Rg2+ Kh8 2. Qxh7+ Kxh7
    3. Rh1#.
12) 1. Re8+ Ka7 2. Ra8+ Kb6
    3. Ra6#.
13) 1. Qb6+ Kc8 2. Qb7+ Kd8
    3. Qd7#.
14) 1. Rh1+ Kg8 2. Rh8+ Kf7
    3. Rf8#.
15) 1. Nb6+ Kb8 2. Qf4+ gxf4
    3. Bxf4#.
16) 1. Bh6+ Ke8 2. Bb5+ Kd8
    3. Rc8#.
17) 1. Bc3+ Kg8 2. Nh6+ Kf8
    3. e7#.
18) 1. Qxg7+ Kxg7 2. f8=Q+ Kh7
    3. Rh1#.
19) 1. Ng6+ hxg6 2. Rh1+ Kg8
    3. Bc4#.
20) 1. f8=Q+ Kxf8 2. h8=Q+ Kf7
    3. Ng5#, or 1. h8=Q+ Kxh8
    2. f8=Q+ Kh7 3. Ng5#.

SECTION IV

SOME DOS AND DON'TS OF CHESS STRATEGY

General

These are rules of thumb to be applied throughout the entire game.

- After every move by your opponent, ask yourself these questions:
    1) Can I capture any of my opponent's pieces to gain material?
    2) What does my opponent want to do?
        a) Am I in check?
        b) Does my opponent want to capture any of my pieces?
        c) Is my opponent threatening a tactical maneuver (i.e., fork, pin, etc.)?
        d) Does my opponent threaten to give checkmate?
- Simplify the position by trading pieces when you are ahead in material.
- Avoid doubling your pawns (placing two pawns on the same file).
- Always try to keep your pawns connected.
- Occupy open file(s) with your rook(s).
- Do not trade a bishop for a knight unless the position is closed (with many pawns and no open lines), or unless you gain some kind of advantage from the exchange.
- Avoid staying in pins.
- Keep your pieces on protected squares as much as possible.

In the Opening

Here are some things to look for in the beginning of the game.

- Control the CENTER (start out by putting at least one center pawn in the center).
- DEVELOP your pieces so that they can attack the center as much as possible.
- Put your king in safety quickly by CASTLING.
- Don't move the same piece twice (unless necessary; i.e., moving away from an attack or recapturing, etc.).
- Don't move your queen out early (usually only after both knights and bishops are developed and the king is safe).
- Connect your rooks by moving out all pieces between them.

In the Middlegame

Below are some things to look for after you have developed all your pieces.

- Look for targets or weaknesses in your opponent's position.
- Make plans based on the targets and your opponent's position.
- When you have an attack going on the opponent's king, avoid trading queens.
- Keep your king safe, usually behind two or three pawns and near the corner.
- Gain a space advantage.

In the Endgame

Here are some things to look for after several pieces (usually including the queens) have been exchanged.

- Try to bring your king toward the center and in play. In the endgame, contrary to the earlier parts of the game, the king should be an active participant, at times even in the attack.

- Try to create passed pawns.
- If you have a passed pawn, advance it. Try to promote your passed pawn to a queen.
- If your opponent has a passed pawn, make sure you can stop it before it reaches the promotion square (or at least make a counter plan).

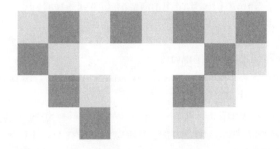

TWO INSTRUCTIVE GAMES

Below are two move-by-move fully analyzed games. These games will show you how to play the opening, the middlegame, and the endgame according to the previously mentioned dos and don'ts. Those were the rules I learned when I started playing chess, and they're the rules I made sure to follow throughout my career. These games also demonstrate how plans are created and used in practice. To make the scores easy to follow, there's a diagram after each move by White.

Game One

White: GM Susan Polgar (2550)
Black: GM Bent Larsen (2560)
Monte Carlo 1994

1. d4

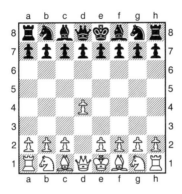

One of the recommended and most logical opening moves. The other classic move, which is just as good, is 1. e4.

1. ... c6

This is not the most common response to White's first move. One of the ideas of this move is to control the d5 square. But Black's real agenda is to wait and see what White wants to do next.

2. c4

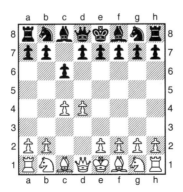

White can choose to attack the d5 square with 2. e4 or 2. c4. These two options lead to completely different types of games.

2. ... d6

Clearing the diagonal for the bishop to develop.

3. Nc3

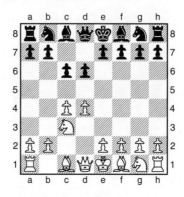

A good developing move to exert more control in the center.

3. ... e5

Not a very popular move. Its purpose is to occupy the center and directly confront the d4 pawn.

4. Nf3

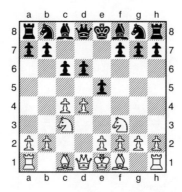

Developing the knight while putting additional pressure on the center.

4. ... Nd7

Developing the knight while giving more protection to the e5 pawn.

5. e4

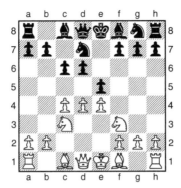

Clearing the diagonal for the other bishop to develop while putting additional presence in the center.

5. ... Ngf6

A normal development move.

6. Be2

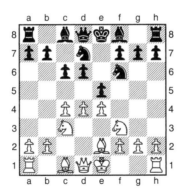

Developing the bishop while clearing the way for the king to castle.

6. ... Be7

Same idea as White. Black develops the bishop and makes room for the king to castle.

7. 0–0

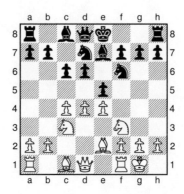

Always remember to castle as soon as possible.

7. ... 0–0

Black also follows the important castling rule.

8. Be3

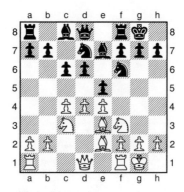

Developing the final minor piece.

8. ... a6

Black has a dilemma. He cannot develop his final minor piece. The knight needs to move out of the way so that the bishop can develop. But the knight has to stay put to protect the e5 pawn.

9. d5

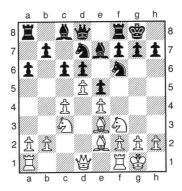

This is a very important positional move. Black has a serious problem due to his lack of space. Black's pieces have very little room to maneuver. Recognizing this, White pushes the d-pawn forward, blocking d6. Now Black will have an even more difficult time freeing his pieces.

9. ... cxd5

An important rule to remember is to try to trade material when your position is tight. Black is trying to do just that.

10. cxd5

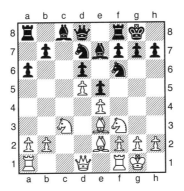

Locking up the center again and keeping the position closed. Why is this important? Because in this position, Black has very little space in which to maneuver. It is hard for Black to find good squares for his pieces and so he has a problem developing his pieces. Because of this, White should continue to close up the position to keep Black's position cramped.

10. ... Ng4

Black is doing the right thing by trying to trade his knight for the bishop. Remember the trading rule!

11. Bd2

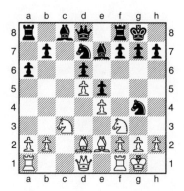

White will not cooperate and allow Black to trade. White will try to avoid trading bishops and to keep the bishop pair.

11. ... Nb6?!

Not a very logical move. The knight is now blocking the b-pawn from advancing. After 11. ... b5 White would try to get a knight to the weakened c6 square with 12. Ne1! Ngf6 13. Nc2 followed by Nb4—c6.

12. h3

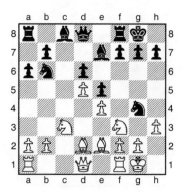

Chasing the knight back and not allowing Black to have room to maneuver.

12. ... Nf6

The only logical retreat.

13. Be3

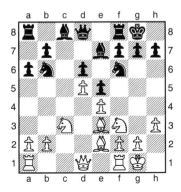

It is now safe for the bishop to go back to its proper position since the Black knight is no longer on g4.

13. ... Ne8

Black is trying to open the position with a possible ... f7–f5.

14. a4

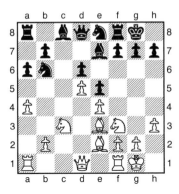

Threatening a4-a5. White continues her plan to limit the mobility of Black's pieces.

14. ... Nd7

Black decides to move the knight away in advance. If he plays ... f5 anyway, White gets a very good position: 14. ... f5 15. a5 Nd7 16. exf5 Rxf5 17. Bd3 Rf7 18. Ne4, with better piece placement for White.

15. a5

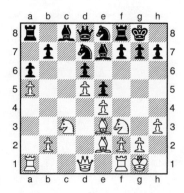

White continues to push forward. Now all of Black's pieces are stuck on the last two ranks.

15. ... g6

Black clears the g7 square for the knight.

16. Nd2

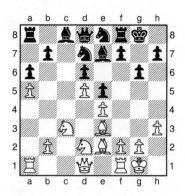

Going for the "hole" on b6.

16. ... Bg5

Black is very persistent in trading pieces to free up some room for his other pieces.

17. Bxg5

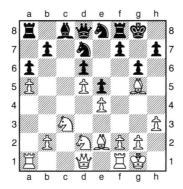

White trades the bishop because there is no way to avoid it.
17. ... Qxg5
The only response.
18. Nc4

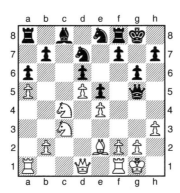

This knight move has two purposes. First, White wants to attack the b6 square; second, he wants to attack the d6 pawn, forcing the knight on e8 to remain buried.
18. ... Rb8
Hoping to open the position with ... b7–b5.

19. Qc1!

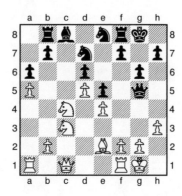

A very strong positional move. The idea is to exchange Black's only active piece.

19. ... Qf4

Black hopes White will take the queen on f4. Black would then recapture with the pawn, freeing the e5 square for his knight. After 19. ... Qxc1 20. Rfxc1 b5 21. axb6 e.p., Nxb6 22. Na5, White's knight gets to the weak c6 square. Somewhat better is 20. ... f5. There is another important point to note. Normally it is not good to have double pawns. The reason is that double pawns are considered weak, vulnerable, and less potent. Pawns are best when they are connected. In this position, Black is willing to accept double pawns in order to free up some space.

20. b4

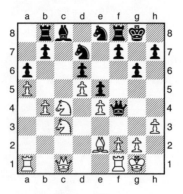

White does not want to help Black free up any space for his pieces. Instead, White continues to gain space while creating a queenside attack.

20. ... h5

Black's pieces are paralyzed. Both rooks and the bishop are stuck. The knight on e8 has to defend the pawn on d6. The knight on d7 is guarding the b6 square.

21. Ra2

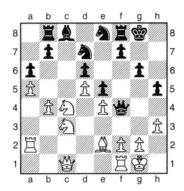

Preparing a possible Ra2–c2. White has a space advantage, more active pieces, and control of the c-file.

21. ... b5

With this move Black gains a little bit of activity, but he has to pay for it by weakening the a-pawn and the c6 square.

22. axb6 e.p.

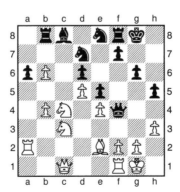

Clearing the a5 square for the knight to get to c6.

22. ... Nxb6

The only recapture that doesn't lost material.

23. Na5!

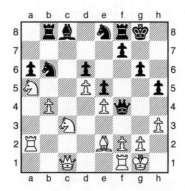

Remember not to trade pieces if the opponent has a tight position. With this move, White avoids the trade and tries to occupy the strong c6 square.

23. ... Kg7

Black still has no good squares for his pieces.

24. Nc6

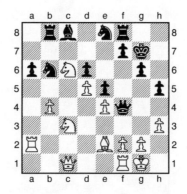

Capturing the powerful c6 square.

24. ... Ra8

Moving away from the attack and protecting the a-pawn.

25. Qxf4

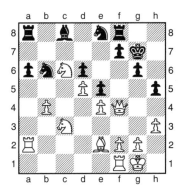

Now White is ready to trade queens, which was Black's only active piece. Black is now completely helpless.

25. ... exf4

The only move.

26. Rc1

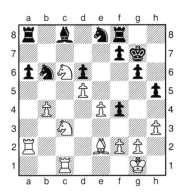

Another rule to remember! Rooks belong on open files.

26. ... Nf6

Black puts pressure on the e-pawn.

27. Rca1!

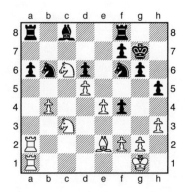

Placing the third attack on the isolated a-pawn, which can no longer be defended.

27. ... Re8

Attacking the pawn on e4 a second time.

28. f3

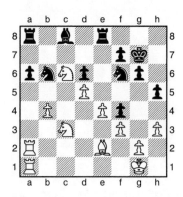

Protecting the e-pawn and stopping any chance for a counterattack.

28. ... Nfd7

With the idea of getting the knight to e5.

29. Bxa6

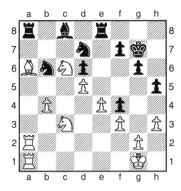

White's first material advantage. Black's queenside now falls apart.

29. ... Bxa6

Black cannot avoid trading bishops.

30. Rxa6

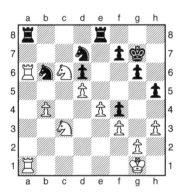

Recapturing the bishop and taking over the a-file.

30. ... Rac8

Another rule of thumb: avoid trading pieces when behind in material. After 30. ... Rxa6 31. Rxa6 Ra8 32. Rxa8 Nxa8, White wins another pawn with 33. Nb5.

31. Nb5

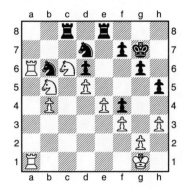

Targeting Black's weak d-pawn.

31. ... Nc4

Protecting the pawn.

32. Nca7

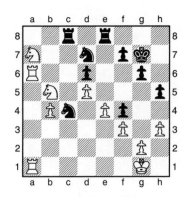

Doubly attacking the rook and the pawn.

32. ... Rb8

Hoping to pin the knight since the pawn on b4 will be exposed after the knight moves.

33. Nxd6

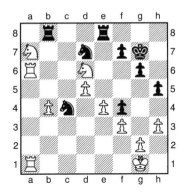

Another weak target has fallen.

33. ... Nxd6

If Black moves the knight or takes the b-pawn, White captures the rook on e8.

34. Rxd6

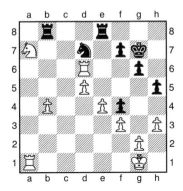

Recapturing the piece while attacking another piece.

34. ... Ne5

Moving the knight to the most logical place, in the center.

35. b5

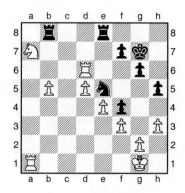

Advancing the passed pawn while giving it protection.

35. ... Rb7

Black wants to double rooks on the b-file to put pressure on the b-pawn.

36. Rda6

To move the rook out of potential danger. After 36. b6 Black can fork with 36. ... Nc4.

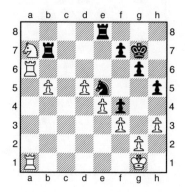

36. ... h4

Black is already in a lost position. The next few moves are just dragging out the end.

37. Rc1

Occupying the other open file.

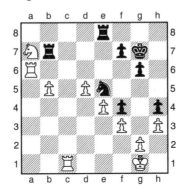

37. ... Nd7

Trying to prevent the advance of the b-pawn.

38. Nc8!

Preparing the advance b6 and threatening to fork the two rooks with 39. Nd6.

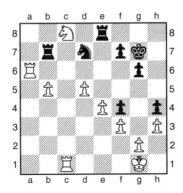

38. ... Rb8

Attacking the knight.

39. Nd6

Avoiding the attack and attacking Black's rook.

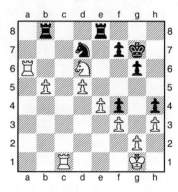

39. ... Rf8

Protecting the f-pawn.

40. Rc7

Attacking the Black knight. Entering the seventh rank with a rook is usually a big accomplishment.

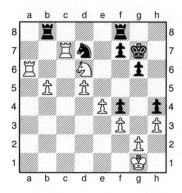

40. ... Ne5
Black avoids the attack.
41. b6
Finally advancing the pawn.

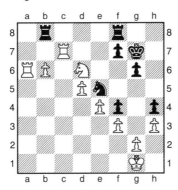

41. ... Ra8
Offering a trade.
42. Rxa8

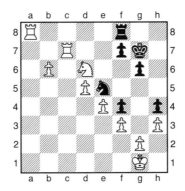

Black resigned. After he recaptures, he will be two pawns down and White's b-pawn will promote soon. A possible continuation would have been: 42. ... Rxa8 43. b7 Rb8 44. Re7 Kf6 45. Re8 Nd7 46. e5+ Kg7 47. e6.

Game Two

White: GM Simen Agdestein (2600)
Black : GM Susan Polgar (2565)
Oslo Rapid, 1996

1. d4

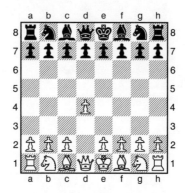

A good first move. It occupies the d4 center square and attacks the e5 center square.

1. ... d5

Same idea as White's. This pawn now occupies the d5 square while attacking the e4 center square.

2. c4

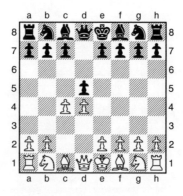

A logical move. The idea is to attack the center pawn. White is not worried that Black might capture the pawn. The reason is that by capturing the pawn, Black would relinquish control of the e4 square. In addition, White would have little trouble recapturing the pawn later since it would be weak and doubled.

2. ... e6

A very logical move to defend the d5 pawn.

3. Nc3

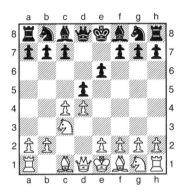

Adding more pressure on the d5 pawn.

3. ... c6

Giving the pawn more protection. This opening is called the Meran Defense. The idea behind Black's last move is to be able to play ... b7-b5 after taking the pawn on c4. Another good choice is to develop with 3. ... Nf6.

4. e3

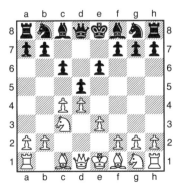

The idea of this move is to open the diagonal for the bishop on f1 so it can protect the c-pawn and develop by moving off the first rank. The move's drawback is that it limits the mobility of the c1 bishop.

4. ... Nf6

A natural developing move, giving more protection to the d5 pawn and strengthening control of the e4 square.

5. b3

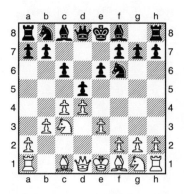

This move makes room for the bishop on c1 to develop by moving to b2, now that the other diagonal is blocked.

5. ... Nbd7

Normal development. Remember, it is wise to keep the pieces close to the center.

6. Bb2

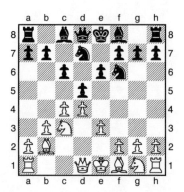

A logical developing move after b3 was played.

6. ... Bd6

Black continues to develop. Now the king is ready to castle.

7. Qc2

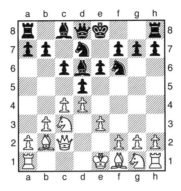

Clearing the way for the king to castle on the queenside.

7. ... 0–0

Remember—castle as soon as you can! This is very important!

8. 0–0–0

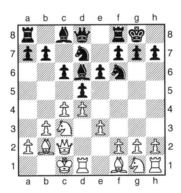

But this is a risky choice by my opponent. The kings have castled on opposite sides, but there is a major difference. In front of the White king there is only one pawn in its ideal initial guarding position (on a2), while Black has all three guard pawns, on f7, g7, and h7.

8. ... a5

Now that the Black king is safe it is time to create a plan. The plan for Black is to start a queenside attack. In order for the attack to be effective, queenside files must be opened. In the next few moves, we see how Black does this.

9. Nf3

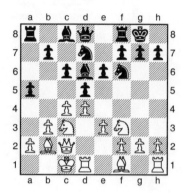

A normal developing move.

9. ... a4

In these situations it is well worth sacrificing a pawn (sometimes even two pawns) in order to open the a-, b-, and c-files and to gain time to attack the enemy king.

10. Nxa4

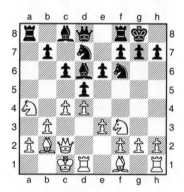

White does not want to double his pawns, which is why he decides to capture the pawn with his knight.

10. ... dxc4

Breaking down the queenside defense.

11. bxc4

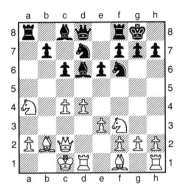

If White takes with the bishop, Black plays 11. ... b5 to fork the two pieces. If White takes the pawn with 11. Qxc4, Black improves his position by bring the knight to the center with 11. ... Nd5.

11. ... b5!

A brilliant move! The idea behind it is to further open the queenside and make the White king a more vulnerable target.

12. cxb5

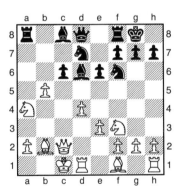

White decides to grab another pawn.

12. ... cxb5

Black succeeds in opening up the queenside files.

13. Bxb5

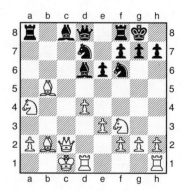

Perhaps White is too greedy. By accepting both pawn sacrifices, White allows Black to open up three critical files for a massive attack against the White king.

13. ... Ba6

This move has two purposes: First, Black wants to eliminate the potentially solid defensive bishop; second, Black wants to clear room for the rook on f8 to maneuver to the queenside to assist in the attack.

14. Bxa6

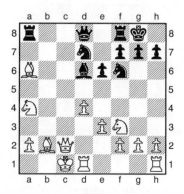

White has little choice but to trade.

14. ... Rxa6

Black has achieved her goal. Now the queen can go behind the rook to support the attack on the a-file.

15. Nd2

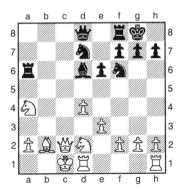

White wants to bring reinforcement to the queenside to protect the king.

15. ... Qa8

Staying on track with the plan to attack.

16. Nc3

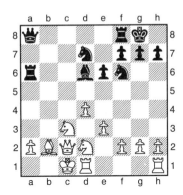

Avoiding the attack while defending the a-pawn.

16. ... Rc8

Placing a devastating double pin on the White queen and king.

17. Ndb1

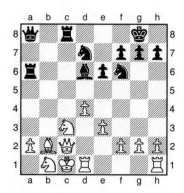

Protecting the pinned knight.

17. ... Rxa2

This move is possible because of the pin on the c3 knight.

18. Rd3

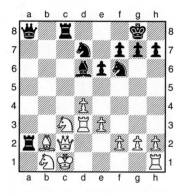

White wants to add reinforcement to the c3 knight. But White is still in big trouble because of the unsafe king.

18. ... Nd5

Adding more fire-power to the queenside attack. The threat is Nb4, forking the queen and rook.

19. Qb3

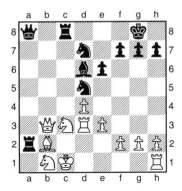

Avoiding the fork.

19. ... Nb4

Attacking the rook and chasing it away from protecting the knight on c3.

20. Rd2

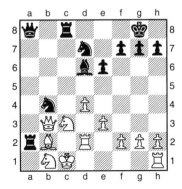

Moving away from the attack while reinforcing the bishop on b2.

20. ... Qxg2

Capturing a pawn while attacking the rook. This move takes away any possible haven for the White king.

21. Rhd1

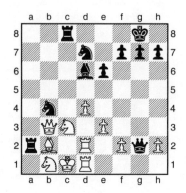

A bad move in a losing position. This move inadvertently traps White's unprotected queen.

21. ... Qb7

The final blow! The serious discovery threat of ... Nd3+ winning the queen is unavoidable. White resigns.

SUPPLEMENT

I

TIPS, ETIQUETTE, AND
HELPFUL ADVICE FOR PLAYERS

- Players should shake hands at the beginning and end of every game.
- Black begins a game by starting the opponent's clock.
- After making your move, press your clock immediately to conserve your time. Use the same hand to press your clock that you use to move your pieces.
- If permitted by tournament rules, Black, as compensation for moving second and thus starting the game with a slight theoretical disadvantage, may choose which chess clock or chess set to use. Black also may choose whether to place the clock on the right or left of the board. One important exception: the digital clock is preferred over the analog clock.
- Make your moves according to the position on the board and ignore the rating of your opponent. Do not overestimate or underestimate your opponents based on their ratings.
- Concentrate! Focus on your game, not on other games. Try not to leave your board unless it is necessary.
- You may not distract any player in any way, especially your opponent.
- It is not ethical to comment on a game that is in progress, whether yours or anyone else's.
- It is not permitted to tell your opponent to move after you have moved.
- The "touch move" rule is always observed in tournament play. If you touch a piece you must move it! When you touch a piece to adjust it, make sure you announce your intention in advance by saying "adjust" or "j'adoube." Otherwise, you may be forced to move the piece you have touched. Also if you have touched one of your oppo-

nent's pieces, and you are able to, you will be forced to capture it by the tournament rules.

- If you are ahead in material, exchange pieces to simplify the position and avoid blunders. If you are behind in material, try not to trade pieces. Try to complicate the position instead.

- Calling check is not required, although you may do so if it does not disturb your opponent or other players. Traditionally, it is regarded as a courtesy and not a rule. Scholastic players are more inclined to call check than advanced players, who generally skip it to acknowledge an opponent's ability to notice when he or she is in check!

- If you wish to offer a draw, make your move first, then offer the draw, then press your clock. Do not offer a draw while your opponent is thinking. That is both illegal and rude. Do not offer a draw repeatedly once it has been rejected. This is disturbing to your opponent.

- If an illegal move is made, summon a tournament director (TD) immediately.

- If a problem or dispute comes up concerning a game in progress, both players should remain calm and immediately stop the clock. Then seek the tournament director. The TD will try to resolve the situation as fairly as possible according to the rules of the United States Chess Federation.

- To resign, a player should politely say "I resign" or politely tip over his or her king. Tipping the king is a sign of surrender.

- There is no time to get upset or angry after a loss in the middle of a tournament. Stay calm. Learn to regroup and concentrate on your next game. It is very important to learn to control your emotions.

- Never gloat over a victory or become upset or hostile following a defeat. It is always best to analyze the game with your opponent after it is over and, if possible, to do so in a different room. Do not disturb other players.

- Players are not required to remind their opponents to press their clock, nor do they need to wait for the opponent to press their clock before making a move (assuming the opponent has already moved). However, my personal rule of sportsmanship is that if I happen to catch my opponent forgetting to press their clock, I would remind them to do so. Under certain circumstances it is important to know how to stop both sides of the chess clock. Find out how to do this before each game. Bathroom breaks, phone calls, etc., are not legitimate reasons to stop the clock.

- Arrive at your game on time. Tardiness is rude. If you arrive more than one hour late you may even be forfeited.
- Do not adjust your pieces on every move. This can be very annoying to your opponent.
- Please do not listen to a Walkman while you are playing. This distracts both you and your opponent.

SUPPLEMENT II

ADVICE FOR PARENTS AND COACHES

- Once the game has started, you may not interrupt, interfere, or talk to your player.
- You may never directly assist any player during a game. If a player raises a hand for assistance, you should immediately summon a TD.
- If you witness an illegal move or position, say nothing. It is the responsibility of the players to bring any complaint to the attention of a TD.
- You are not permitted to say anything if a player oversteps the time limit. Only the players themselves can claim a win on time.
- When a player loses a game, you must refrain from getting upset or angry or showing negative emotions. Young players need support and encouragement more than ever after a loss. They do not need scolding. You should try to help players stay calm and relaxed for the rest of the tournament.
- You may help your players find their correct table and board before each round.
- You should supervise your player between rounds. It is not the responsibility of the TD or organizer to mind your children between rounds.
- You should keep your player from distracting other players during and between rounds.
- Players should try to conserve their energy between rounds so they can be fresh for the next game.
- You should always encourage your player to practice good sportsmanship at all times, especially after losing a game.
- Official chess tournaments are smoke free.

- You should view your players' games only from behind them or in the aisle to avoid eye contact with them.
- Keep a distance between yourself and your player. In some large tournaments, you may not even be allowed in the playing room during a game.
- If you see a player or a team playing the wrong opponent, you should notify a TD immediately.
- Only tournament officials can record information on wall charts. Parents, coaches, and players should never write on them. However, players may record their results on the pairing charts. If you notice an error on the wall chart, bring it to the attention of a TD.
- You should make sure that your players' results are reported in a timely manner.
- If you detect that a prize has been erroneously awarded after the end of a tournament, bring this to the attention of a TD.

Great Titles from the McKay Chess Library

Title Information	Level of Play *
The Art of Defense in Chess ISBN: 0-679-14108-1 $15.95/C$23.95	I
The Art of Positional Play ISBN: 0-8129-3475-X $15.95/C$23.95	I-A
Basic Chess Endings ISBN: 0-8129-3493-8 $24.95/C$37.95	All Levels
Best Lessons of a Chess Coach ISBN: 0-8129-2265-4 $16.95/C$24.95	B-I
The Chess Advantage in Black and White ISBN: 0-8129-3571-3 $18.95/C$28.95	I-A
Chess Fundamentals ISBN: 0-679-14004-2 $14.95/C$22.95	B
Chess Openings the Easy Way ISBN: 0-8129-3498-9 $15.95/C$23.95	All Levels
The Ideas Behind Chess Openings ISBN: 0-8129-1756-1 $13.95/C$21.00	B-I
The Inner Game of Chess ISBN: 0-8129-2291-3 $16.95/C$24.95	I-A
Judgment & Planning in Chess ISBN: 0-679-14325-4 $12.95/C$19.95	I-A
The Middlegame in Chess ISBN: 0-8129-3484-9 $18.95/C$28.95	I-A
Modern Chess Openings 14th ed. ISBN: 0-8129-3084-3 $29.95/C$44.95	I-A
Modern Chess Strategy ISBN: 0-679-14022-0 $15.00/C$23.00	I-A
Pawn Structure Chess ISBN: 0-8129-2529-7 $16.00/C$24.00	I-A
United States Chess Federation Official Rules *of Chess, 5th ed.* ISBN: 0-8129-3559-4 $18.95/C$28.95	No Rating

*Key to levels of play: (B) = beginner; (I) = Intermediate; (A) = Advanced

Available at your local bookseller.
To order by phone, call 1-800-733-3000.

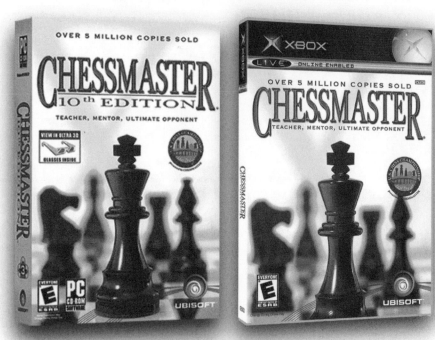